Unforgettable writing
about the many faces of war . . .

"THE BURNING" *by* **EUDORA WELTY**
Two Southern ladies react to the burning of their
home by Yankees with a horrific courage . . . and an
act of fatal desperation.

"CHICKAMAUGA" *by* **THOMAS WOLFE**
A ninety-five-year-old Confederate veteran remembers
the strange battle of Stone Mountain, the tragedy of
Shiloh, and the soul-changing experience of
Chickamauga.

**"MY GRANDMOTHER MILLARD AND GENERAL
BEDFORD FORREST AND THE BATTLE OF HARRYKIN
CREEK"** *by* **WILLIAM FAULKNER**
Part farce, part drama, this tale adds an unexpected
twist to a wartime romance and an enterprising
matriarch determined to save the family's valuables.

"PILLAR OF FIRE" *by* **SHELBY FOOTE**
A disfigured Union officer carries out a campaign of
retribution along the Mississippi and burns down an
old man's home with chilling results.

"SECOND INAUGURAL" *by* **ABRAHAM LINCOLN**
This succinct address, written with the same
impassioned, pain-filled voice heard in the Gettysburg
Address, reminds the nation of the rightness of the
Union's cause.

CHICKAMAUGA

and other Civil War stories

EDITED BY SHELBY FOOTE

Delta
Trade Paperbacks

A Delta Book
Published by
Bantam Dell
a division of
Random House, Inc.

Library of Congress Cataloging in Publication Data

Chickamauga and other Civil War stories / edited by Shelby Foote.
      p.   cm.
    Contents: Introduction—Provisional inaugural / Jefferson Davis—A young soldier's first battle / Stephen Crane—The night of Chancellorsville / F. Scott Fitzgerald—Chickamauga / Thomas Wolfe—An occurrence at Owl Creek Bridge / Ambrose Bierce—My Grandmother Millard and General Bedford Forrest and the Battle of Harrykin Creek / William Faulkner—Fish-Hook Gettysburg / Stephen Vincent Benét—The burning / Eudora Welty—Pillar of fire / Shelby Foote—Homecoming / John O'Hara—A private history of a campaign that failed / Mark Twain—Second inaugural / Abraham Lincoln.
    ISBN 0-385-31100-1
    1. United States—History—Civil War, 1861-1865—Fiction. 2. War stories, American. I. Foote, Shelby.
PS648.C54C45 1993
813'.0108358—dc20   93-879
                                                            CIP

Interior design by Jeremiah B. Lighter
Manufactured in the United States of America
Published simultaneously in Canada
November 1993
10   9   8
RRC

CONTENTS

Introduction

In the summer of 1862, following McClellan's mauled retreat from the gates of Richmond, James Russell Lowell's reply to his editor's request for a poem was that he was "clear down to the bottom of the well, where I see the Truth too near to make verses of." Similarly, Harriet Beecher Stowe—saluted by Lincoln in person as "the little lady who started this big war"—responded, when asked why she had not written a wartime sequel to *Uncle Tom's Cabin*: "Who could write fiction when life was so imperious and terrible?" Nathaniel Hawthorne, on the other hand, felt "mentally and physically languid" under pressure from the conflict, and though he died while Grant was outmaneuvering Lee down in Virginia, just short of a year before the finish, he did manage to produce an essay titled "Chiefly About War Matters" in which he confessed that "the Present, the Immediate, the Actual, has proved too potent for me. It takes away not only my scanty faculty, but even my desire for imaginative composition, and leaves me sadly content to scatter a thousand peaceful fantasies upon the hurricane that is sweeping us all along with it, possibly, into a Limbo where our nation and its polity may be as literally the fragments of a scattered dream as my unwritten Romance."

Nor did the end of the war provide any sudden correction of this blockage. Two years after Appomattox, William Dean Howells—assistant editor of the *Atlantic Monthly* at thirty, soon to be editor-in-chief, and for the next forty years the acknowledged dean of American letters—declared that the war "has laid upon our literature a charge under which it has staggered very lamely." Crane's *The Red Badge of Courage*, published a generation later in 1895, was the exception that proved the rule; the sluice gate opened only to close again. Indeed, Howell's complaint is nearly as valid today as it was when he made it, just over 125 years ago.

In this country, historical fiction has in general been left to second-raters and hired brains, and this is particularly true of those who have chosen the Civil War as a major subject. Aside from Crane, our best fiction writers have given it mere incidental attention or none at all. Hemingway is a case in point; so is Henry James. This is regrettable on several counts, especially to those who would understand our nation by learning just what happened during that blood-drenched era—good and bad things, both in abundance—to make us what we are. Facts we have had and are having in ever greater numbers, perhaps a glut, through the years leading up to and away from the Sumter centennial, when biographies, overall explications, and brochures came pouring in a torrent from the presses and binderies. Yet there is a multifaceted truth outside the facts—beyond them, so to speak, or hidden inside them—and of this we have had all too little, because in this respect our novelists have let us down. "I would rather have *The Iliad*," a recent translator of Homer has said, "than a whole shelf of Bronze Age war reports." So too, no doubt, would we; but there is no American *Iliad*, *John Brown's Body* notwithstanding.

This collection is an attempt, on a small scale, to examine what has been done to lessen the gap our best creative writers left unfilled in dealing with the four-year segment of history connecting Jefferson Davis's Provisional Inaugural at Montgomery in mid-February of 1861 and Abraham Lincoln's Second Inaugural at Washington in early March of 1865. Scarcity made the task of selection difficult in one sense and easy in another. As it turned out—Ambrose Bierce being the earli-

est author represented—the writing span was reduced
to the near-seventy years (1891–1960) that fell between
Tales of Soldiers and Civilians and John O'Hara's *Ourselves
to Know*, from which I snipped the single page I sometimes think is perhaps the best single page in the whole
collection.

However that may be, the test for inclusion applied
in each case was neither the subject nor the event de-
scribed, no matter how desirable or attractive from a
historical point of view, but rather the quality of the
writing itself—a criterion that cost me the northern real-
ist John W. De Forest, along with the southern romanti-
cist John Esten Cooke, as well as a good many others on
both sides. Only this, it seems to me—the way and tone
of the telling—can make a story memorable or true in
the real sense. The *Monitor–Merrimac* duel in Hampton
Roads, the headlong charge up Missionary Ridge, the
death of Pat Cleburne at Franklin, Grant in his rumpled
clothes at Appomattox: these and a host of other occur-
rences, worthy as they are in their own right, are not
here because I could not find them measured up to, or
even approximated, in the writing.

What we have in their stead is a series of events
totally unlike the ones mentioned above: a coachload of
whores on a siding during a great battle in Virginia, an
old man remembering his particular corner of a bloody
field in Georgia, a pioneer being suffocated in the back-
wash of war in the Mississippi delta, a young slave girl
wading into the Big Black River with the gathered
bones of the child she bore her dead master's missing
son, a gallant Confederate lieutenant losing the seat of
his trousers as he rescues a fair damsel from the wreck-
age of an outhouse, a spy's thoughts as his Union cap-
tors break his neck below a bridge in Alabama, the bale-
ful welcome-home of a pair of shattered Pennsylvania

veterans, a New York farm boy looking forward to the test of combat and then running when it comes, and Mark Twain on the eve of his skedaddle. (The one exception is Benét's panoramic view of Fish-Hook Gettysburg; but I had to go to epic poetry to find it.)

These are what remain after the winnowing: a sorry-enough array, on the face of it, out of an era that is supposed to have been, and in large part was, wildly romantic. Yet, such is the power and glory of art, by transmutation they are no less noble, even as events, than the ones that had to be left out because good writers failed to take them up. Of the ten authors represented in these pages, half are Northern, half are Southern, and if any bias favoring the latter is suspected or detected, I can promise you'll find precious little moonlight and no magnolias at all. As for the inclusion of a story by the compiler, I can only say that, for one thing, I rather think it belongs here, and for another—which gladdened the heart of the publisher—it was free.

Otherwise no apology is called for, as anyone who reads ahead will see. Even the incidental attention of writers like Fitzgerald and Wolfe produces for us an insight we otherwise would lack. The hookers on the day coach, the old man looking back through time to Chickamauga: these show us dimensions of that tragic confrontation we might never have known if something had not drawn these two writers' attention, even incidentally. And if selections predominate toward the near end of that seven-decade span, this too can be taken not only as a sign that, in one regard at least, American writing has improved in the main with age, but also as an indication, or in any case grounds for hope, that the best is yet to come.

Provisional Inaugural

JEFFERSON DAVIS

Montgomery, Alabama
February 18, 1861

Friends and Fellow-Citizens: Our present political position has been achieved in a manner unprecedented in the history of nations. It illustrates the American idea that government rests on the consent of the governed, and that it is the right of the people to alter or abolish them at will whenever they become destructive of the ends for which they were established. The declared purpose of the compact of the Union from which we have withdrawn was to "establish justice, insure domestic tranquillity, provide for the common defense, promote the general welfare, and secure the blessings of liberty to ourselves and our posterity"; and when, in the judgment of the sovereign States composing this Confederacy, it has been perverted from the purposes for which it was ordained, and ceased to answer the ends for which it was established, a peaceful appeal to the ballot-box declared that, so far as they are concerned, the Government created by that compact should cease to exist.

In this they merely asserted the right which the Declaration of Independence of July 4, 1776 defined to be "inalienable." Of the time and occasion of its exercise they as sovereigns were the final judges, each for itself. The impartial and enlightened verdict of mankind will vindicate the rectitude of our conduct; and He who knows the hearts of men will judge of the sincerity with which we have labored to preserve the Government of our fathers in its spirit.

An agricultural people, whose chief interest is the export of commodities required in every manufacturing country, our true policy is peace, and the freest trade which our necessities will permit. It is alike our interest and that of all those to whom we would sell, and from whom we would buy, that there should be the fewest practicable restrictions upon the interchange of these commodities. There can, however, be but little rivalry between ours and any manufacturing or navigating community, such as the Northeastern States of the American Union. It must follow, therefore, that mutual interest will invite to good-will and kind offices on both parts. If, however, passion or lust of dominion should cloud the judgment or inflame the ambition of those States, we must prepare to meet the emergency and maintain, by the final arbitrament of the sword, the position which we have assumed among the nations of the earth.

We have entered upon the career of independence, and it must be inflexibly pursued. Through many years of controversy with our late associates of the Northern States, we have vainly endeavored to secure tranquillity and obtain respect for the rights to which we were entitled. As a necessity, not a choice, we have resorted to the remedy of separation, and henceforth our energies must be directed to the conduct of our own affairs, and the perpetuity of the Confederacy which we have formed. If a just perception of mutual interest shall permit us peaceably to pursue our separate political career, my most earnest desire will have been fulfilled. But if this be denied to us, and the integrity of our territory and jurisdiction be assailed, it will but remain for us with firm resolve to appeal to arms and invoke the blessing of Providence on a just cause.

Should reason guide the action of the Government from which we have separated, a policy so detrimental to the civilized world, the Northern States included, could not be dictated by even the strongest desire to inflict injury upon us;

but, if the contrary should prove true, a terrible responsibility will rest upon it, and the suffering of millions will bear testimony to the folly and wickedness of our aggressors.

It is joyous in the midst of perilous times to look around upon a people united in heart, where one purpose of high resolve animates and actuates the whole; where the sacrifices to be made are not weighed in the balance against honor and right and liberty and equality. Obstacles may retard, but they cannot long prevent, the progress of a movement sanctified by its justice and sustained by a virtuous people. Reverently let us invoke the God of our Fathers to guide and protect us in our efforts to perpetuate the principles which by His blessing they were able to vindicate, establish, and transmit to their posterity. With the continuance of His favor ever gratefully acknowledged, we may hopefully look forward to success, to peace, and to prosperity.

A Young Soldier's First Battle

STEPHEN CRANE

At nightfall the column broke into regimental pieces, and the fragments went into the fields to camp. Tents sprang up like strange plants. Camp fires, like red, peculiar blossoms, dotted the night.

The youth kept from intercourse with his companions as much as circumstances would allow him. In the evening he wandered a few paces into the gloom. From this little distance the many fires, with the black forms of men passing to and fro before the crimson rays, made weird and satanic effects.

He lay down in the grass. The blades pressed tenderly against his cheek. The moon had been lighted and was hung in a treetop. The liquid stillness of the night enveloping him made him feel vast pity for himself. There was a caress in the soft winds; and the whole mood of the darkness, he thought, was one of sympathy for himself in his distress.

He wished, without reserve, that he was at home again making the endless rounds from the house to the barn, from the barn to the fields, from the fields to the barn, from the barn to the house. He remembered he had often cursed the brindle cow and her mates, and had sometimes flung milking stools. But, from his present point of view, there was a halo of happiness about each of their heads, and he would have sacrificed all the brass buttons on the continent to have been enabled to return to them. He told himself that he was not formed for a soldier. And he mused seriously upon the radical differences between himself and those men who were dodging imp-like around the fires.

As he mused thus he heard the rustle of grass, and, upon turning his head, discovered the loud soldier. He called out, "Oh, Wilson!"

The latter approached and looked down. "Why hello, Henry; is it you? What you doing here?"

"Oh, thinking," said the youth.

The other sat down carefully lighted his pipe. "You're getting blue, my boy. You're looking thundering peaked. What the dickens is wrong with you?"

"Oh, nothing," said the youth.

The loud soldier launched then into the subject of the anticipated fight. "Oh, we've got 'em now!" As he spoke his boyish face was wreathed in a gleeful smile, and his voice had an exultant ring. "We've got 'em now. At last, by the eternal thunders, we'll lick 'em good!"

"If the truth was known," he added, more soberly, *"they've* licked *us* about every clip up to now; but this time—this time, we'll lick 'em good!"

"I thought you was objecting to this march a little while ago," said the youth coldly.

"Oh, it wasn't that," explained the other. "I don't mind marching, if there's going to be fighting at the end of it. What I hate is this getting moved here and moved there, with no good coming of it, as far as I can see, excepting sore feet and damned short rations."

"Well, Jim Conklin says we'll get aplenty of fighting this time."

"He's right for once, I guess, though I can't see how it come. This time we're in for a big battle, and we've got the best end of it, certain sure. Gee rod! how we will thump 'em!"

He arose and began to pace to and fro excitedly. The thrill of his enthusiasm made him walk with an elastic step. He was sprightly, vigorous, fiery in his belief in success. He looked into the future with clear, proud eye, and he swore with the air of an old soldier.

The youth watched him for a moment in silence. When he finally spoke his voice was as bitter as dregs. "Oh, you're going to do great things, I s'pose!"

The loud soldier blew a thoughtful cloud of smoke from his pipe. "Oh, I don't know," he remarked with dignity; "I don't know. I s'pose I'll do as well as the rest. I'm going to try like thunder." He evidently complimented himself upon the modesty of this statement.

"How do you know you won't run when the time comes?" asked the youth.

"Run?" said the loud one; "run?—of course not!" He laughed.

"Well," continued the youth, "lots of good-a-'nough men have thought they was going to do great things before the fight, but when the time come they skedaddled."

"Oh, that's all true, I s'pose," replied the other; "but I'm not going to skedaddle. The man that bets on my running will lose his money, that's all." He nodded confidently.

"Oh, shucks!" said the youth. "You ain't the bravest man in the world, are you?"

"No, I ain't," exclaimed the loud soldier indignantly; "and I didn't say I was the bravest man in the world, neither. I said I was going to do my share of fighting—that's what I said. And I am, too. Who are you, anyhow? You talk as if you thought you was Napoleon Bonaparte." He glared at the youth for a moment, and then strode away.

The youth called in a savage voice after his comrade: "Well, you needn't git mad about it!" But the other continued on his way and made no reply.

He felt alone in space when his injured comrade had disappeared. His failure to discover any mite of resemblance in their view points made him more miserable than before. No one seemed to be wrestling with such a terrific personal problem. He was a mental outcast.

He went slowly to his tent and stretched himself on a blanket by the side of the snoring tall soldier. In the darkness he saw visions of a thousand-tongued fear that would babble at his back and cause him to flee, while others were going coolly about their country's business. He admitted that he would not be able to cope with this monster. He felt that every nerve in his body would be an ear to hear the voices, while other men would remain stolid and deaf.

And as he sweated with the pain of these thoughts, he could hear low, serene sentences. "I'll bid five." "Make it six." "Seven." "Seven goes."

He stared at the red, shivering reflection of a fire on the white wall of his tent until, exhausted and ill from the monotony of his suffering, he fell asleep.

2

When another night came the columns, changed to purple streaks, filed across two pontoon bridges. A glaring fire wine-tinted the waters of the river. Its rays, shining upon the moving masses of troops, brought forth here and there sudden gleams of silver and gold. Upon the other shore a dark and mysterious range of hills was curved against the sky. The insect voices of the night sang solemnly.

After this crossing the youth assured himself that at any moment they might be suddenly and fearfully assaulted from the caves of the lowering woods. He kept his eyes watchfully upon the darkness.

But his regiment went unmolested to a camping place, and its soldiers slept the brave sleep of wearied men. In the morning they were routed out with early energy, and hustled along a narrow road that led deep into the forest.

It was during this rapid march that the regiment lost many of the marks of a new command.

The men had begun to count the miles upon their fingers, and they grew tired. "Sore feet an' damned short rations, that's all," said the loud soldier. There was perspiration and grumblings. After a time they began to shed their knapsacks. Some tossed them unconcernedly down; others hid them carefully, asserting their plans to return for them at some convenient time. Men extricated themselves from thick shirts. Presently few carried anything but their necessary clothing, blankets, haversacks, canteens, and arms and ammunition.

There was a sudden change from the ponderous infantry of theory to the light and speedy infantry of practice. The regiment, relieved of a burden, received a new impetus. But there was much loss of valuable knapsacks, and, on the whole, very good shirts.

But the regiment was not yet veteranlike in appearance. Veteran regiments in the army were likely to be very small aggregations of men. Once, when the command had first come to the field, some perambulating veterans, noting the length of their column, had accosted them thus: "Hey, fellers, what brigade is that?" And when the men had replied that they formed a regiment and not a brigade, the older soldiers had laughed and said, "O Gawd!"

Also, there was too great a similarity in the hats. The hats of a regiment should properly represent the

history of headgear for a period of years. And, more-
over, there were no letters of faded gold speaking from
the colors. They were new and beautiful, and the color-
bearer habitually oiled the pole.

Presently the army again sat down to think. The
odor of the peaceful pines was in the men's nostrils. The
sounds of monotonous axe blows rang through the forest, and the insects, nodding upon their perches,
crooned like old women. The youth returned to his theory of a blue demonstration.

One gray dawn, however, he was kicked in the leg
by the tall soldier, and then, before he was entirely
awake he found himself running down a wood road in
the midst of men who were panting from the first effects
of speed. His canteen banged rhythmically upon his
thigh, and his haversack bobbed softly. His musket
bounced a trifle from his shoulder at each stride and
made his cap feel uncertain upon his head.

He could hear the men whisper jerky sentences:
"Say—what's all this—about?" "What th' thunder—we
—skedaddlin' this way fer?" "Billie—keep off m' feet.
Yeh run—like a cow." And the loud soldier's shrill
voice could be heard: "What th' devil they in sich a
hurry for?"

The youth thought the damp fog of early morning
moved from the rush of a great body of troops. From
the distance came a sudden spatter of firing.

He was bewildered. As he ran with his comrades
he strenuously tried to think, but all he knew was that if
he fell down those coming behind would tread upon
him. All his faculties seemed to be needed to guide him
over and past obstructions. He felt carried along by a
mob.

The sun spread disclosing rays, and, one by one,
regiments burst into view like armed men just born of

the earth. The youth perceived that the time had come. He was about to be measured. For a moment he felt in the face of his great trial like a babe, and the flesh over his heart seemed very thin. He seized time to look about him calculatingly.

But he instantly saw that it would be impossible for him to escape from the regiment. It inclosed him. And there were iron walls of tradition and law on four sides. He was in a moving box.

As he perceived this fact it occurred to him that he had never wished to come to the war. He had not enlisted of his free will. He had been dragged by the merciless government. And now they were taking him out to be slaughtered.

The regiment slid down a bank and wallowed across a little stream. The mournful current moved slowly on, and from the water, shaded black, some white bubble eyes looked at the men.

As they climbed the hill on the farther side artillery began to boom. Here the youth forgot many things as he felt a sudden impulse of curiosity. He scrambled up the bank with a speed that could not be exceeded by a blood-thirsty man.

He expected a battle scene.

There were some little fields girted and squeezed by a forest. Spread over the grass and in among the tree trunks, he could see knots and waving lines of skirmishers who were running hither and thither and firing at the landscape. A dark battle line lay upon a sunstruck clearing that gleamed orange color. A flag fluttered.

Other regiments floundered up the bank. The brigade was formed in line of battle, and after a pause started slowly through the woods in the rear of the receding skirmishers, who were continually melting into the scene to appear again farther on. They were always busy as bees, deeply absorbed in their little combats.

The youth tried to observe everything. He did not use care to avoid trees and branches, and his forgotten feet were constantly knocking against stones or getting entangled in briers. He was aware that these battalions with their commotions were woven red and startling into the gentle fabric of softened greens and browns. It looked to be a wrong place for a battlefield.

The skirmishers in advance fascinated him. Their shots into thickets and at distant and prominent trees spoke to him of tragedies—hidden, mysterious, solemn.

Once the line encountered the body of a dead soldier. He lay upon his back staring at the sky. He was dressed in an awkward suit of yellowish brown. The youth could see that the soles of his shoes had been worn to the thinness of writing paper, and from a great rent in one the dead foot projected piteously. And it was as if fate had betrayed the soldier. In death it exposed to his enemies that poverty which in life he had perhaps concealed from his friends.

The ranks opened covertly to avoid the corpse. The invulnerable dead man forced a way for himself. The youth looked keenly at the ashen face. The wind raised the tawny beard. It moved as if a hand were stroking it. He vaguely desired to walk around and around the body and stare; the impulse of the living to try to read in dead eyes the answer to the Question.

3

During the march the ardor which the youth had acquired when out of view of the field rapidly faded to nothing. His curiosity was quite easily satisfied. If an intense scene had caught him with its wild swing as he came to the top of the bank, he might have gone roaring on. This advance upon Nature was too calm. He had opportunity to reflect. He had time in which to wonder about himself and to attempt to probe his sensations.

Absurd ideas took hold upon him. He thought that he did not relish the landscape. It threatened him. A coldness swept over his back, and it is true that his trousers felt to him that they were not fit for his legs at all.

A house standing placidly in distant fields had to him an ominous look. The shadows of the woods were formidable. He was certain that in this vista there lurked fierce-eyed hosts. The swift thought came to him that the generals did not know what they were about. It was all a trap. Suddenly those close forests would bristle with rifle barrels. Ironlike brigades would appear in the rear. They were all going to be sacrificed. The generals were stupid. The enemy would presently swallow the whole command. He glared about him, expecting to see the stealthy approach of his death.

He thought that he must break from the ranks and harangue his comrades. They must not all be killed like pigs; and he was sure it would come to pass unless they were informed of these dangers. The generals were idiots to send them marching into a regular pen. There was but one pair of eyes in the corps. He would step forth and make a speech. Shrill and passionate words came to his lips.

The line, broken into moving fragments by the ground, went calmly on through fields and woods. The youth looked at the men nearest him, and saw, for the most part, expressions of deep interest, as if they were investigating something that had fascinated them. One or two stepped with overvaliant airs as if they were already plunged into war. Others walked as upon thin ice. The greater part of the untested men appeared quiet and absorbed. They were going to look at war, the red animal—war, the blood-swollen god. And they were deeply engrossed in this march.

As he looked the youth gripped his outcry at his throat. He saw that even if the men were tottering with fear they would laugh at his warning. They would jeer him, and, if practicable, pelt him with missiles. Admitting that he might be wrong, a frenzied declamation of the kind would turn him into a worm.

He assumed, then, the demeanor of one who knows that he is doomed alone to unwritten responsibilities. He lagged, with tragic glances at the sky.

He was surprised presently by the young lieutenant of his company, who began heartily to beat him with a sword, calling out in a loud and insolent voice: "Come, young man, get up into the ranks there. No skulking'll do here." He mended his pace with suitable haste. And he hated the lieutenant, who had no appreciation of fine minds. He was a mere brute.

After a time the brigade was halted in the cathedral light of a forest. The busy skirmishers were still popping. Through the aisles of the wood could be seen the floating smoke from their rifles. Sometimes it went up in little balls, white and compact.

During this halt many men in the regiment began erecting tiny hills in front of them. They used stones, sticks, earth, and anything they thought might turn a bullet. Some built comparatively large ones, while others seemed content with little ones.

This procedure caused a discussion among the men. Some wished to fight like duelists, believing it to be correct to stand erect and be, from their feet to their foreheads, a mark. They said they scorned the devices of the cautious. But the others scoffed in reply, and pointed to the veterans on the flanks who were digging at the ground like terriers. In a short time there was quite a barricade along the regimental fronts. Directly, however, they were ordered to withdraw from that place.

This astounded the youth. He forgot his stewing over the advance movement. "Well, then, what did they march us out here for?" he demanded of the tall soldier. The latter with calm faith began a heavy explanation, although he had been compelled to leave a little protection of stones and dirt to which he had devoted much care and skill.

When the regiment was aligned in another position, each man's regard for his safety caused another line of small intrenchments. They ate their noon meal behind a third one. They were moved from this one also. They were marched from place to place with apparent aimlessness.

The youth had been taught that a man became another thing in a battle. He saw his salvation in such a change. Hence this waiting was an ordeal to him. He was in a fever of impatience. He considered that there was denoted a lack of purpose on the part of the generals. He began to complain to the tall soldier. "I can't stand this much longer," he cried. "I don't see what good it does to make us wear out our legs for nothin'." He wished to return to camp, knowing that this affair was a blue demonstration; or else to go into a battle and discover that he had been a fool in his doubts, and was, in truth, a man of traditional courage. The strain of present circumstances he felt to be intolerable.

The philosophical tall soldier measured a sandwich of cracker and pork and swallowed it in a nonchalant manner. "Oh, I suppose we must go reconnoitering around the country jest to keep 'em from getting too close, or to develop 'em, or something."

"Huh!" said the loud soldier.

"Well," cried the youth, still fidgeting, "I'd rather do anything, 'most than go tramping 'round the country all day doing no good to nobody and jest tiring ourselves out."

"So would I," said the loud soldier. "It ain't right. I tell you if anybody with any sense was a-runnin' this army it—"

"Oh, shut up!" roared the tall private. "You little fool. You little damn' cuss. You ain't had that there coat and them pants on for six months, and yet you talk as if—"

"Well, I wanta do some fighting anyway," interrupted the other. "I didn't come here to walk. I could 'ave walked to home—'round an' 'round the barn, if I jest wanted to walk."

The tall one, red-faced, swallowed another sandwich as if taking poison in despair.

But gradually, as he chewed, his face became again quiet and contented. He could not rage in fierce argument in the presence of such sandwiches. During his meals he always wore an air of blissful contemplation of the food he had swallowed. His spirit seemed then to be communing with the viands.

He accepted new environment and circumstance with great coolness, eating from his haversack at every opportunity. On the march he went along with the stride of a hunter, objecting to neither gait nor distance. And he had not raised his voice when he had been ordered away from three little protective piles of earth and stone, each of which had been an engineering feat worthy of being made sacred to the name of his grandmother.

In the afternoon the regiment went out over the same ground it had taken in the morning. The landscape then ceased to threaten the youth. He had been close to it and become familiar with it.

When, however, they began to pass into a new region, his old fears of stupidity and incompetence reassailed him, but this time he doggedly let them babble. He was occupied with his problem, and in his desperation he concluded that the stupidity did not greatly matter.

Once he thought he had concluded that it would be better to get killed directly and end his troubles. Regarding death thus out of the corner of his eye, he conceived it to be nothing but rest, and he was filled with a momentary astonishment that he should have made an extraordinary commotion over the mere matter of getting killed. He would die; he would go to some place where he would be understood. It was useless to expect appreciation of his profound and fine senses from such men as the lieutenant. He must look to the grave for comprehension.

The skirmish fire increased to a long clattering sound. With it was mingled far-away cheering. A battery spoke.

Directly the youth would see the skirmishers running. They were pursued by the sound of musketry fire. After a time, the hot, dangerous flashes of the rifles were visible. Smoke clouds went slowly and insolently across the fields like observant phantoms. The din became crescendo, like the roar of an oncoming train.

A brigade ahead of them and on the right went into action with a rending roar. It was as if it had exploded. And thereafter it lay stretched in the distance behind a long gray wall, that one was obliged to look twice at to make sure that it was smoke.

The youth, forgetting his neat plan of getting killed, gazed spellbound. His eyes grew wide and busy with the action of the scene. His mouth was a little ways open.

Of a sudden he felt a heavy and sad hand laid upon his shoulder. Awakening from his trance of observation, he turned and beheld the loud soldier.

"It's my first and last battle, old boy," said the latter, with intense gloom. He was quite pale, and his girlish lip was trembling.

"Eh?" murmured the youth in great astonishment.

"It's my first and last battle, old boy," continued the loud soldier. "Something tells me—"

"What?"

"I'm a gone coon this first time, and—and I w-want you to take these here things—to—my—folks." He ended in a quavering sob of pity for himself. He handed the youth a little packet done up in a yellow envelope.

"Why, what the devil—" began the youth again.

But the other gave him a glance as from the depths of a tomb, and raised his limp hand in a prophetic manner and turned away.

4

The brigade was halted in the fringe of a grove. The men crouched among the trees and pointed their restless guns out at the fields. They tried to look beyond the smoke.

Out of this haze they could see running men. Some shouted information and gestured as they hurried.

The men of the new regiment watched and listened eagerly while their tongues ran on in gossip of the battle. They mouthed rumors that had flown like birds out of the unknown.

"They say Perry has been driven in with big loss."

"Yes, Carrott went t' th' hospital. He said he was

sick. That smart lieutenant is commanding 'G' Company. Th' boys say they won't be under Carrott no more if they all have t' desert. They allus knew he was a————."

"Hannises' batt'ry is took."

"It ain't either. I saw Hannises' batt'ry off on th' left not more'n fifteen minutes ago."

"Well—"

"Th' general, he ses he is goin' t' take th' hull command of th' 304th when we go inteh action, an' then he ses we'll do sech fightin' as never another one reg'ment done."

"They say we're catchin' it over on th' left. They say th' enemy driv' our line inteh a devil of a swamp an' took Hannises' batt'ry."

"No sech thing. Hannises' batt'ry was 'long here 'bout a minute ago."

"That young Hasbrouck, he makes a good off'cer. He ain't afraid 'a nothin'."

"I met one of th' 148th Maine boys an' he ses his brigade fit th' hull rebel army fer four hours over on th' turnpike road 'n killed about five thousand of 'em. He ses one more sech fight as that an' th' war'll be over."

"Bill wasn't scared either. No, sir! It wasn't that. Bill ain't a-gittin' scared easy. He was jest mad, that's what he was. When that feller trod on his hand, he up an' sed that he was willin' t' give his hand t' his country, but he be dumbed if he was goin' t' have every dumb bushwhacker in th' kentry walkin' 'round on it. So he went t' th' hospital disregardless of t' fight. Three fingers was crunched. Th' dern doctor wanted t' amputate 'm, an' Bill, he raised a helluva row, I hear. He's a funny feller."

The din in front swelled to a tremendous chorus. The youth and his fellows were frozen to silence. They could see a flag that tossed in the smoke angrily. Near it were the blurred and agitated forms of troops. There came a turbulent stream of men across the fields. A battery changing position at a frantic gallop scattered the stragglers right and left.

A shell screaming like a storm banshee went over the huddled heads of the reserves. It landed in the grove, and exploding redly flung the brown earth. There was a little shower of pine needles.

Bullets began to whistle among the branches and nip at the trees. Twigs and leaves came sailing down. It was as if a thousand axes, wee and invisible, were being wielded. Many of the men were constantly dodging and ducking their heads.

The lieutenant of the youth's company was shot in the hand. He began to swear so wondrously that a nervous laugh went along the regimental line. The officer's profanity sounded conventional. It relieved the tightened senses of the new men. It was as if he had hit his fingers with a tack hammer at home.

He held the wounded member carefully away from his side so that the blood would not drip upon his trousers.

The captain of the company, tucking his sword under his arm, produced a handkerchief and began to bind with it the lieutenant's wound. And they disputed as to how the binding should be done.

The battle flag in the distance jerked about madly. It seemed to be struggling to free itself from an agony. The billowing smoke was filled with horizontal flashes.

Men running swiftly emerged from it. They grew in numbers until it was seen that the whole command was fleeing. The flag suddenly sank down as if dying. Its motion as it fell was a gesture of despair.

Wild yells came from behind the walls of smoke. A

sketch in gray and red dissolved into a moblike body of men who galloped like wild horses.

The veteran regiments on the right and left of the 304th immediately began to jeer. With the passionate song of the bullets and the banshee shrieks of shells were mingled loud catcalls and bits of facetious advice concerning places of safety.

But the new regiment was breathless with horror. "Gawd! Saunders got crushed!" whispered the man at the youth's elbow. They shrank back and crouched as if compelled to await a flood.

The youth shot a swift glance along the blue ranks of the regiment. The profiles were motionless, carven; and afterward he remembered that the color sergeant was standing with his legs apart, as if he expected to be pushed to the ground.

The following throng went whirling around the flank. Here and there were officers carried along on the stream like exasperated chips. They were striking about them with their swords and with their left fists, punching every head they could reach. They cursed like highwaymen.

A mounted officer displayed the furious anger of a spoiled child. He raged with his head, his arms, and his legs.

Another, the commander of the brigade, was galloping about bawling. His hat was gone and his clothes were awry. He resembled a man who has come from bed to go to a fire. The hoofs of his horse often threatened the heads of the running men, but they scampered with singular fortune. In this rush they were apparently all deaf and blind. They heeded not the largest and longest of the oaths that were thrown at them from all directions.

Frequently over this tumult could be heard the

grim jokes of the critical veterans; but the retreating men apparently were not even conscious of the presence of an audience.

The battle reflection that shone for an instant in the faces on the mad current made the youth feel that forceful hands from heaven would not have been able to have held him in place if he could have got intelligent control of his legs.

There was an appalling imprint upon these faces. The struggle in the smoke had pictured an exaggeration of itself on the bleached cheeks and in the eyes with one wild desire.

The sight of this stampede exerted a floodlike force that seemed able to drag sticks and stones and men from the ground. They of the reserves had to hold on. They grew pale and firm, and red and quaking.

The youth achieved one little thought in the midst of this chaos. The composite monster which had caused the other troops to flee had not then appeared. He resolved to get a view of it, and then, he thought, he might very likely run better than the best of them.

5

There were moments of waiting. The youth thought of the village street at home before the arrival of the circus parade on a day in the spring. He remembered how he had stood, a small, thrillful boy, prepared to follow the dingy lady upon the white horse, or the band in its faded chariot. He saw the yellow road, the lines of expectant people, and the sober houses. He particularly remembered an old fellow who used to sit upon a cracker box in front of the store and feign to despise such exhibitions. A thousand details of color and form surged in his mind. The old fellow upon the cracker box appeared in middle prominence.

Someone cried, "Here they come!"

There was rustling and muttering among the men. They displayed a feverish desire to have every possible cartridge ready to their hands. The boxes were pulled around into various positions, and adjusted with great care. It was as if seven hundred new bonnets were being tried on.

The tall soldier, having prepared his rifle, produced a red handkerchief of some kind. He was engaged in knotting it about his throat with exquisite attention to its position, when the cry was repeated up and down the line in a muffled roar of sound.

"Here they come! Here they come!" Gun locks clicked.

Across the smoke-infested fields came a brown swarm of running men who were giving shrill yells. They came on, stooping and swinging their rifles at all angles. A flag, tilted forward, sped near the front.

As he caught sight of them, the youth was momentarily startled by a thought that perhaps his gun was not loaded. He stood trying to rally his faltering intellect so that he might recollect the moment when he had loaded, but he could not.

A hatless general pulled his dripping horse to a stand near the colonel of the 304th. He shook his fist in the other's face. "You've got to hold 'em back!" he shouted savagely; "you've got to hold 'em back!"

In his agitation the colonel began to stammer. "A-all r-right, General, all right, by Gawd! We-we'll do our we-we'll d-d-do—do our best, General." The general made a passionate gesture and galloped away. The colonel, perchance to relieve his feelings, began to scold like a wet parrot. The youth, turning swiftly to make sure that the rear was unmolested, saw the commander regarding his men in a highly resentful manner, as if he regretted above everything his association with them.

The man at the youth's elbow was mumbling, as if to himself, "Oh, we're in for it now! Oh, we're in for it now!"

The captain of the company had been pacing excitedly to and fro in the rear. He coaxed in schoolmistress fashion, as to a congregation of boys with primers. His talk was an endless repetition. "Reserve your fire, boys—don't shoot till I tell you—save your fire—wait till they get close up—don't be damned fools—"

Perspiration streamed down the youth's face, which was soiled like that of a weeping urchin. He frequently, with a nervous movement, wiped his eyes with his coat sleeve. His mouth was still a little ways open.

He got the one glance at the foe-swarming field in front of him, and instantly ceased to debate the question of his piece being loaded. Before he was ready to begin—before he had announced to himself that he was about to fight—he threw the obedient, well-balanced rifle into position and fired a first wild shot. Directly he was working at his weapon like an automatic affair.

He suddenly lost concern for himself, and forgot to look at a menacing fate. He became not a man but a member. He felt that something of which he was a part—a regiment, an army, a cause, or a country—was in a crisis. He was welded into a common personality which was dominated by a single desire. For some moments he could not flee, no more than a little finger can commit a revolution from a hand.

If he had thought the regiment was about to be annihilated perhaps he could have amputated himself from it. But its noise gave him assurance. The regiment was like a firework that, once ignited, proceeds superior to circumstances until its blazing vitality fades. It wheezed and banged with a mighty power. He pictured the ground before it as strewn with the discomfited.

There was a consciousness always of the presence of his comrades about him. He felt the subtle battle brotherhood more potent even than the cause for which they were fighting. It was a mysterious fraternity born of the smoke and danger of death.

He was at a task. He was like a carpenter who has made many boxes, making still another box, only there was furious haste in his movements. He, in his thought, was careering off in other places, even as the carpenter who, as he works, whistles and thinks of his friend or his enemy, his home or a saloon. And these jolted dreams were never perfect to him afterward, but remained a mass of blurred shapes.

Presently he began to feel the effects of the war atmosphere—a blistering sweat, a sensation that his eyeballs were about to crack like hot stones. A burning roar filled his ears.

Following this came a red rage. He developed the acute exasperation of a pestered animal, a well-meaning cow worried by dogs. He had a mad feeling against his rifle, which could only be used against one life at a time. He wished to rush forward and strangle with his fingers. He craved a power that would enable him to make a world-sweeping gesture and brush all back. His impotency appeared to him, and made his rage into that of a driven beast.

Buried in the smoke of many rifles, his anger was directed not so much against the men whom he knew were rushing toward him, as against the swirling battle phantoms which were choking him, stuffing their smoke robes down his parched throat. He fought frantically for respite for his senses, for air, as a babe being smothered attacks the deadly blankets.

There was a blare of heated rage mingled with a certain expression of intentness on all faces. Many of the men were making low-toned noises with their mouths, and these subdued cheers, snarls, imprecations, prayers, made a wild, barbaric song that went as an undercurrent of sound, strange and chantlike, with the resounding chords of the war march. The man at the youth's elbow was babbling. In it there was something soft and tender, like the monologue of a babe. The tall soldier was swearing in a loud voice. From his lips came a black procession of curious oaths. Of a sudden another broke out in a querulous way, like a man who has mislaid his hat. "Well, why don't they support us? Why don't they send supports? Do they think—"

The youth in his battle sleep heard this as one who dozes hears.

6

There was singular absence of heroic poses. The men, bending and surging in their haste and rage, were in every impossible attitude. The steel ramrods clanked and clanged with incessant din as the men pounded them furiously into the hot rifle barrels. The flaps of the cartridge boxes were all unfastened, and bobbed idiotically with each movement. The rifles, once loaded, were jerked to the shoulder and fired without apparent aim into the smoke or at one of the blurred and shifting forms which, upon the field before the regiment, had been growing larger and larger like puppets under a magician's hands.

The officers, at their intervals, rearward, neglected to stand in picturesque attitudes. They were bobbing to and fro, roaring directions and encouragements. The dimensions of their howls were extraordinary. They expended their lungs with prodigal wills. And often they nearly stood upon their heads in their anxiety to observe the enemy on the other side of the tumbling smoke.

The lieutenant of the youth's company had encountered a soldier who had fled screaming at the first volley of his comrades. Behind the lines these two were acting a little isolated scene. The man was blubbering and staring with sheeplike eyes at the lieutenant, who had seized him by the collar and was pommeling him. He drove him back into the ranks with many blows. The soldier went mechanically, dully, with his animal-like eyes upon the officer. Perhaps there was to him a divinity expressed in the voice of the other—stern, hard, with no reflection of fear in it. He tried to reload his gun, but his shaking hands prevented. The lieutenant was obliged to assist him.

The men dropped here and there like bundles.

The captain of the youth's company had been killed in an early part of the action. His body lay stretched out in the position of a tired man resting, but upon his face there was an astonished and sorrowful look, as if he thought some friend had done him an ill turn. The babbling man was grazed by a shot that made the blood stream widely down his face. He clasped both hands to his head. "Oh!" he said, and ran. Another grunted suddenly as if he had been struck by a club in the stomach. He sat down and gazed ruefully. In his eyes there was a mute, indefinite reproach. Further up the line a man, standing behind a tree, had had his knee joint splintered by a ball. Immediately he had dropped his rifle and gripped the tree with both arms. And there he remained, clinging desperately and crying for assistance, that he might withdraw his hold upon the tree.

At last an exultant yell went along the quivering line. The firing dwindled from an uproar to a last vindictive popping. As the smoke slowly eddied away, the youth saw that the charge had been repulsed. The enemy were scattered into reluctant groups. He saw a man climb to the top of the fence, straddle the rail, and fire a parting shot. The waves had receded, leaving bits of dark debris upon the ground.

Some in the regiment began to whoop frenziedly. Many were silent. Apparently they were trying to contemplate themselves.

After the fever had left his veins, the youth thought that at last he was going to suffocate. He became aware of the foul atmosphere in which he had been struggling. He was grimy and dripping like a laborer in a foundry. He grasped his canteen and took a long swallow of the warmed water.

A sentence with variations went up and down the line. "Well, we've helt 'em back. We've helt 'em back; derned if we haven't." The men said it blissfully, leering at each other with dirty smiles.

The youth turned to look behind him and off to the right and off to the left. He experienced the joy of a man who at last finds leisure in which to look about him.

Underfoot there were a few ghastly forms motionless. They lay twisted in fantastic contortions. Arms were bent and heads were turned in incredible ways. It seemed that the dead men must have fallen from some great height to get into such positions. They looked to be dumped out upon the ground from the sky.

From a position in the rear of the grove a battery was throwing shells over it. The flash of the guns startled the youth at first. He thought they were aimed directly at him. Through the trees he watched the black figures of the gunners as they worked swiftly and intently. Their labor seemed a complicated thing. He wondered how they could remember its formula in the midst of confusion.

The guns squatted in a row like savage chiefs. They argued with abrupt violence. It was a grim pow-wow. Their busy servants ran hither and thither.

A small procession of wounded men were going drearily toward the rear. It was a flow of blood from the torn body of the brigade.

To the right and to the left were the dark lines of other troops. Far in front he thought he could see lighter masses protruding in points from the forest. They were suggestive of unnumbered thousands.

Once he saw a tiny battery go dashing along the line of the horizon. The tiny riders were beating the tiny horses.

From a sloping hill came the sounds of cheerings and clashes. Smoke welled slowly through the leaves.

Batteries were speaking with thunderous oratorical effort. Here and there were flags, the red in the stripes dominating. They splashed bits of warm color upon the dark lines of troops.

The youth felt the old thrill at the sight of the emblem. They were like beautiful birds strangely undaunted in a storm.

As he listened to the din from the hillside, to a deep pulsating thunder that came from afar to the left, and to the lesser clamors which came from many directions, it occurred to him that they were fighting too, over there, and over there, and over there. Heretofore he had supposed that all the battle was directly under his nose.

As he gazed around him the youth felt a flash of astonishment at the blue, pure sky and the sun gleaming on the trees and fields. It was surprising that Nature had gone tranquilly on with her golden process in the midst of so much devilment.

7

The youth awakened slowly. He came gradually back to a position from which he could regard himself. For moments he had been scrutinizing his person in a dazed way as if he had never before seen himself. Then he picked up his cap from the ground. He wriggled in his jacket to make a more comfortable fit, and kneeling, replaced his shoe. He thoughtfully mopped his reeking features.

So it was all over at last! The supreme trial had been passed. The red, formidable difficulties of war had been vanquished.

He went into an ecstasy of self-satisfaction. He had the most delightful sensations of his life. Standing as if apart from himself, he viewed that last scene. He perceived that the man who had fought thus was magnificent.

He felt that he was a fine fellow. He saw himself even with those ideals which he had considered as far beyond him. He smiled in deep gratification.

Upon his fellows he beamed tenderness and good will. "Gee! ain't it hot, hey?" he said affably to a man who was polishing his streaming face with his coat sleeves.

"You bet!" said the other, grinning sociably. "I never seen sech dumb hotness." He sprawled out luxuriously on the ground. "Gee, yes! An' I hope we don't have no more fightin' till a week from Monday."

There were some handshakings and deep speeches with men whose features were familiar, but with whom the youth now felt the bonds of tied hearts. He helped a cursing comrade to bind up a wound of the shin.

But, of a sudden, cries of amazement broke out along the ranks of the new regiment. "Here they come ag'in! Here they come ag'in!" The man who had sprawled upon the ground started up and said, "Gosh!"

The youth turned quick eyes upon the field. He discerned forms begin to swell in masses out of a distant wood. He again saw the tilted flag speeding forward.

The shells, which had ceased to trouble the regiment for a time, came swirling again, and exploded in the grass or among the leaves of the trees. They looked to be strange war flowers bursting into fierce bloom.

The men groaned. The luster faded from their eyes. Their smudged countenances now expressed a profound dejection. They moved their stiffened bodies slowly, and watched in sullen mood the frantic approach of the enemy. The slaves toiling in the temple of this god began to feel rebellion at his harsh tasks.

They fretted and complained each to each. "Oh, say, this is too much of a good thing! Why can't somebody send us supports?"

"We ain't never goin' to stand this second banging. I didn't come here to fight the hull damn' rebel army."

There was one who raised a doleful cry. "I wish Bill Smithers had trod on my hand, insteader me treddin' on his'n." The sore joints of the regiment creaked as it painfully floundered into position to repulse.

The youth stared. Surely, he thought, this impossible thing was not about to happen. He waited as if he expected the enemy to suddenly stop, apologize, and retire bowing. It was all a mistake.

But the firing began somewhere on the regimental line and ripped along in both directions. The level sheets of flame developed great clouds of smoke that tumbled and tossed in the mild wind near the ground for a moment, and then rolled through the ranks as through a gate. The clouds were tinged an earthlike yellow in the sunrays and in the shadows were a sorry blue. The flag was sometimes eaten and lost in this mass of vapor, but more often it projected, sun-touched, resplendent.

Into the youth's eyes there came a look that one can see in the orbs of a jaded horse. His neck was quivering with nervous weakness, and the muscles of his arms felt numb and bloodless. His hands, too, seemed large and awkward, as if he was wearing invisible mittens. And there was a great uncertainty about his knee joints.

The words that comrades had uttered previous to the firing began to recur to him. "Oh, say, this is too much of a good thing! What do they take us for—why don't they send supports? I didn't come here to fight the hull damned rebel army."

He began to exaggerate the endurance, the skill, and the valor of those who were coming. Himself reeling from exhaustion, he was astonished beyond measure at such persistency. They must be machines of steel. It was very gloomy struggling against such affairs, wound up perhaps to fight until sundown.

He slowly lifted his rifle and, catching a glimpse of the thickspread field, he blazed at a cantering cluster. He stopped then and began to peer as best he could through the smoke. He caught changing views of the ground covered with men who were all running like pursued imps, and yelling.

To the youth it was an onslaught of redoubtable dragons. He became like the man who lost his legs at the approach of the red and green monster. He waited in a sort of horrified, listening attitude. He seemed to shut his eyes and wait to be gobbled.

A man near him, who up to this time had been working feverishly at his rifle, suddenly stopped and ran with howls. A lad whose face had borne an expression of exalted courage, the majesty of him who dares give his life, was, at an instant, smitten abject. He blanched like one who has come to the edge of a cliff at midnight and is suddenly made aware. There was a revelation. He, too, threw down his gun and fled. There was no shame in his face. He ran like a rabbit.

Others began to scamper away through the smoke. The youth turned his head, shaken from his trance by this movement as if the regiment was leaving him behind. He saw the few fleeting forms.

He yelled then with fright, and swung about. For a moment, in the great clamor, he was like a proverbial chicken. He lost the direction of safety. Destruction threatened him from all points.

Directly he began to speed toward the rear in great leaps. His rifle and cap were gone. His unbuttoned coat bulged in the wind. The flap of his cartridge box bobbed wildly, and his canteen, by its slender cord, swung out behind. On his face was all the horror of those things which he imagined.

The Night of Chancellorsville

F. SCOTT FITZGERALD

I tell you I didn't have any notion what I was getting into or I wouldn't of gone down there. They can have their army—it seems to me they were all acting like a bunch of yellow bellies. But my friend Nell said to me:

"Look here, Nora, Philly is as dead as Baltimore and we've got to eat this summer." She'd just got a letter from a girl that said they were living fine down there in "old Virginia." The soldiers were getting big pay offs and figuring maybe they'd stay there all summer, till the Johnny Rebs gave up. They got their pay regular too, and a good clean-looking girl could ask—well, I forget now, because after what happened to us I guess you can't expect me to remember anything.

I've always been used to decent treatment—somehow when I meet a man, no matter how fresh he is in the beginning, he comes to respect me in the end and I've never had things done to me like some girls, getting left in a strange town or had my purse stolen.

Well, I started to tell you how I went down to the army in "old Virginia." Never again! Wait till you hear.

I'm used to travelling nice—once when I was a little girl my daddy took me on the cars to Baltimore—we lived in York, Pa.—and we couldn't have been more comfortable; we had pillows and the men came through with baskets of oranges and apples, you know, singing out:

"Want to buy some oranges or apples—or beer."

You know what they sell—but I never took any beer because—

Oh I know, I'll go on—You only want to talk about the war, like all you men. But if that's their idea what a war is—

Well, they stuck us all in one car and a fresh guy took our tickets and winked and said:

"Oh, you're going down to Hooker's army."

The lights was terrible in the car, smoky and not cleaned so everything looked sort of yellow. And say that car was so old it was falling to pieces.

There must have been forty girls in it, a lot of them from Baltimore and Philly. Only there were three or four that weren't gay—I mean they were more, oh you know, rich people that sat up front; every once in a while an officer would pop in his head from the next car and ask them if they wanted anything. I was in the seat behind with Nell and we heard him whisper:

"You're in pretty terrible company but we'll be there in a few hours and we'll go right to headquarters, and I'll promise you solid comfort."

I never will forget that night. None of us had any food except some girls behind us had some sausage and bread, and they gave us what they had left. There was a spigot you turned but no water came out. After about two hours, stopping every two minutes it seemed to me, a couple of lieutenants, loaded to the gills, came in from the next car and offered Nell and me some whiskey out of a bottle. Nell took some and I pretended to and they sat on the side of our seats. One of them started to make up to her but just then the officer that had spoken to the women, pretty high up I guess, a major or a general, came back again and asked:

"You all right? Anything I can do?"

One of the ladies kind of whispered to him, and he

turned to the drunk that was talking to Nell and made him go back in the other car. After that there was only one officer with us; he wasn't really so drunk, just feeling sick.

"This certainly is a jolly looking gang," he says. "It's good you can hardly see them in this light. They look as if their best friend just died."

"What if they do," Nell answered back. "How would you look yourself if you come all the way from Philly and then climbed in a car like this?"

"I come all the way from the Seven Days, Sister," he answered; pretty soon he left and said he'd try and get us some water or coffee, which was what we wanted.

The car kept rocking and it made us both feel funny. Some of the girls was sick and some was sound asleep on each other's shoulders.

"Hey, where is this army?" Nell demanded. "Down in Mexico?"

I was kind of half asleep myself by that time and didn't answer.

The next thing I knew I was woke up by a storm, the car was stopped again and I said, "It's raining."

"Raining!" said Nell. "That's cannon—they're having a battle."

"Oh. Well, after *this* ride I don't care who wins."

It seemed to be getting louder all the time, but out the windows you couldn't see anything on account of the mist.

In about half an hour another officer came in the car—he looked pretty messy as if he'd just crawled out of bed: his coat was still unbuttoned and he kept hitching up his trousers as if he didn't have any suspenders.

"All you ladies outside," he said, "we need this car for the wounded."

"What?"

"Hey!"

"We paid for our tickets, didn't we?"

"I don't care. We need all the cars for the wounded and the other cars are about filled up."

"Hey! We didn't come down to fight in any battle!"

"It doesn't matter what you came down for—you're in a battle, a hell of a battle."

I was scared I can tell you. I thought maybe the Rebs would capture us and send us down to one of those prisons you hear about where they starve you to death unless you sing Dixie all the time and kiss niggers.

"Hurry up now!"

But another officer had come in who looked more nice.

"Stay where you are, ladies," he said, and then he said to the officer, "What do you want to do, leave them standing on the siding! If Sedgewick's Corps is broken like they say the Rebs may come up in this direction!" Some of the girls began crying out loud. "These are northern women after all."

"These are—"

"Oh shut up—go back to your command. I'm detailed to this transportation job, and I'm taking these girls to Washington with us."

I thought they were going to hit each other but they both walked off together, and we sat wondering what we were going to do.

What happened next I don't quite remember. The cannon were sometimes very loud and then sometimes more far away, but there was firing of shots right near us and a girl down the car had her window smashed. I heard a whole bunch of horses gallop by our windows but I still couldn't see anything.

This went on for half an hour—gallopings and more shots. We couldn't tell how far away but they sounded like up by the engine.

Then it got quiet and two guys came into our car—we all knew right away they were rebels, not officers, just plain private ones with guns. One had on a brown blouse and one a blue blouse and I was surprised because I thought they always wore grey. They were disgusting looking and very dirty; one had a big pot of jam he'd smeared all over his face and the other had a box of crackers.

"Hi, ladies."

"What you gals doin' down here?"

"Kaint you see, Steve, this is old Joe Hooker's staff."

"Reckin we ought to take 'em back to the General?"

They talked outlandish like that—I could hardly understand they talked so funny.

One of the girls got hysterical, she was so scared and that made them kind of shy. They were just kids I guess, under those beards, and one of them tipped his hat or whatever the old thing was:

"We're not fixin' to hurt you."

At that moment there was a whole bunch more shooting down by the engine and the rebs turned and ran. We were glad I can tell you.

Then about fifteen minutes later in came one of our officers. This was another new one.

"You better duck down!" he shouted to us, "they may shell this train. We're starting you off as soon as we load two more ambulances on board."

Half of us was on the floor already. The rich women sitting ahead of Nell and me went up into the car ahead where the wounded were—I heard one of them say to see if they could do anything. Nell thought she'd look in too, but she came back holding her nose— she said it smelled awful in there.

It was lucky she didn't go in because two of the girls did try and see if they could help, but the nurses sent them right back, as if they was dirt under their feet.

After I don't know how long the train began to move. A soldier came in and poured the oil out of all our lights except one and took it into the wounded car, so now we could hardly see at all.

If the trip down was slow the trip back was terrible. The wounded began groaning and we could hear in our car, so nobody couldn't get a decent sleep. We stopped everywhere.

When we got in Washington at last there was a lot of people in the station and they were all anxious about what had happened to the army, but I said you can search me. All I wanted was my little old room and my little old bed. I never been treated like that in my life. One of the girls said she was going to write to President Lincoln about it.

And in the papers next day they never said anything about how our train got attacked or about us girls at all! Can you beat it?

Chickamauga

THOMAS WOLFE

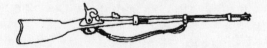

On the seventh day of August, 1861, I was nineteen years of age. If I live to the seventh day of August this year I'll be ninety-five years old. And the way I feel this mornin' I intend to live. Now I guess you'll have to admit that that's goin' a good ways back.

I was born up at the Forks of the Toe River in 1842. Your grandpaw, boy, was born at the same place in 1828. His father, and mine, too, Bill Pentland—your great-grandfather, boy—moved into that region way back right after the Revolutionary War and settled at the Forks of Toe. The real Indian name fer hit was Estatoe, but the white men shortened hit to Toe, and hit's been known as Toe River ever since.

Of course hit was all Indian country in those days. I've heared that the Cherokees helped Bill Pentland's father build the first house he lived in, where some of us was born. I've heared, too, that Bill Pentland's grandfather came from Scotland back before the Revolution, and that thar was three brothers. That's all the Pentlands that I ever heared of in this country. If you ever meet a Pentland anywheres you can rest assured he's descended from one of those three.

Well, now, as I was tellin' you, upon the seventh day of August, 1861, I was nineteen years of age. At seven-thirty in the mornin' of that day I started out from home and walked the whole way in to Clingman. Jim Weaver had come over from Big Hickory where he lived the night before and stayed with me. And now he went along with me. He was the best friend I had. We had growed up alongside of each other: now we was to march alongside of each other fer many a long and weary mile—how many neither of us knowed that mornin' when we started out.

Hit was a good twenty mile away from where we lived to Clingman, and I reckon young folks nowadays would consider twenty mile a right smart walk. But fer people in those days hit wasn't anything at all. All of us was good walkers. Why Jim Weaver could keep goin' without stoppin' all day long.

Jim was big and I was little, about the way you see me now, except that I've shrunk up a bit, but I could keep up with him anywhere he went. We made hit into Clingman before twelve o'clock—hit was a hot day, too —and by three o'clock that afternoon we had both joined up with the Twenty-ninth. That was my regiment from then on, right on to the end of the war. Anyways, I was an enlisted man that night, the day that I was nineteen years of age, and I didn't see my home again fer four long years.

Your Uncle Bacchus, boy, was already in Virginny: we knowed he was thar because we'd had a letter from him. He joined up right at the start with the Fourteenth. He'd already been at First Manassas and I reckon from then on he didn't miss a big fight in Virginny fer the next four years, except after Antietam where he got wounded and was laid up fer four months.

Even way back in those days your Uncle Bacchus had those queer religious notions that you've heared about. The Pentlands are good people, but everyone who ever knowed 'em knows they can go queer on religion now and then. That's the reputation that they've always had. And that's the way Back was. He was a Russellite even in those days: accordin' to his notions the world was comin' to an end and he was goin' to be right in on hit when hit happened. That was the way he had hit figgered out. He was always prophesyin' and predictin' even back before the war, and when the war came, why Back just knowed that this was hit.

Why law! He wouldn't have missed that war fer anything. Back didn't go to war because he wanted to kill Yankees. He didn't want to kill nobody. He was as tender-hearted as a baby and as brave as a lion. Some fellers told hit on him later how they'd come on him at Gettysburg, shootin' over a stone wall, and his rifle bar'l had got so hot he had to put hit down and rub his hands on the seat of his pants because they got so blistered. He was singin' hymns, they said, with tears a-streamin' down his face—that's the way they told hit, anyway—and every time he fired he'd sing another verse. And I reckon he killed plenty because when Back had a rifle in his hands he didn't miss.

But he was a good man. He didn't want to hurt a fly. And I reckon the reason that he went to war was because he thought he'd be at Armageddon. That's the way he had hit figgered out, you know. When the war came, Back said: "Well, this is hit, and I'm a-goin' to be thar. The hour has come," he said, "when the Lord is goin' to set up His Kingdom here on earth and separate the sheep upon the right hand and the goats upon the left—jest like hit was predicted long ago—and I'm a-goin' to be thar when hit happens."

Well, we didn't ask him which side *he* was goin' to be on, but we all knowed which side without havin' to ask. Back was goin' to be on the *sheep* side—that's the way *he* had hit figgered out. And that's the way he had hit figgered out right up to the day of his death ten years ago. He kept prophesyin' and predictin' right up to the end. No matter what happened, no matter what mistakes he made, he kept right on predictin'. First he said the war was goin' to be the Armageddon day. And when that didn't happen he said hit was goin' to come along in the eighties. And when hit didn't happen then he moved hit up to the nineties. And when the war broke out in 1914 and the whole world had to go, why Bacchus knowed that that was hit.

And no matter how hit all turned out, Back never would give in or own up he was wrong. He'd say he'd made a mistake in his figgers somers, but that he'd found out what hit was and that next time he'd be right. And that's the way he was up to the time he died.

I had to laugh when I heared the news of his death, because of course, accordin' to Back's belief, after you die nothin' happens to you fer a thousand years. You jest lay in your grave and sleep until Christ comes and wakes you up. So that's why I had to laugh. I'd a-give anything to've been there the next mornin' when Back woke up and found himself in heaven. I'd've give anything just to've seen the expression on his face. I may have to wait a bit but I'm goin' to have some fun with him when I see him. But I'll bet you even then he won't give in. He'll have some reason fer hit, he'll try to argue he was right but that he made a little mistake about hit somers in his figgers.

But Back was a good man—a better man than Bacchus Pentland never lived. His only failin' was the failin' that so many Pentlands have—he went and got queer religious notions and he wouldn't give them up.

Well, like I say then, Back was in the Fourteenth. Your Uncle Sam and Uncle George was with the Seventeenth, and all three of them was in Lee's army in Virginny. I never seed nor heared from either Back or Sam fer the next four years. I never knowed what had happened to them or whether they was dead or livin'

until I got back home in '65. And of course I never
heared from George again until they wrote me after
Chancellorsville. And then I knowed that he was dead.
They told hit later when I came back home that hit took
seven men to take him. They asked him to surrender.
And then they had to kill him because he wouldn't be
taken. That's the way he was. He never would give up.
When they got to his dead body they told how they had
to crawl over a whole heap of dead Yankees before they
found him. And then they knowed hit was George.
That's the way he was, all right. He never would give
in.

He is buried in the Confederate cemetery at Richmond, Virginny. Bacchus went through thar more than
twenty years ago on his way to the big reunion up at
Gettysburg. He hunted up his grave and found out
where he was.

That's where Jim and me thought that we'd be too.
I mean with Lee's men, in Virginny. That's where we
thought that we was goin' when we joined. But, like I'm
goin' to tell you now, hit turned out different from the
way we thought.

Bob Saunders was our Captain; L. C. McIntyre our
Major; and Leander Briggs the Colonel of our regiment.
They kept us thar at Clingman fer two weeks. Then they
marched us into Altamont and drilled us fer the next
two months. Our drillin' ground was right up and
down where Parker Street now is. In those days thar
was nothing thar but open fields. Hit's all built up now.
To look at hit today you'd never know thar'd ever been
an open field thar. But that's where hit was, all right.

Late in October we was ready and they moved us
on. The day they marched us out, Martha Patton came
in all the way from Zebulon to see Jim Weaver before
we went away. He'd known her fer jest two months;

he'd met her the very week we joined up and I was with him when he met her. She came from out along Cane River. Thar was a camp revival meetin' goin' on outside of Clingman at the time, and she was visitin' this other gal in Clingman while the revival lasted; and that was how Jim Weaver met her. We was walkin' along one evenin' toward sunset and we passed this house where she was stayin' with this other gal. And both of them was settin' on the porch as we went past. The other gal was fair, and she was dark: she had black hair and eyes, and she was plump and sort of little, and she had the pertiest complexion, and the pertiest white skin and teeth you ever seed; and when she smiled there was a dimple in her cheeks.

Well, neither of us knowed these gals, and so we couldn't stop and talk to them, but when Jim saw the little 'un he stopped short in his tracks like he was shot, and then he looked at her so hard she had to turn her face. Well, then, we walked on down the road a piece and Jim stopped and turned and looked again, and when he did, why, sure enough, he caught her lookin' at him too. And then her face got red—she looked away again.

Well, that was where she landed him. He didn't say a word, but Lord! I felt him jerk there like a trout upon the line—and I knowed right then and thar she had him hooked. We turned and walked on down the road a ways, and then he stopped and looked at me and said:

"Did you see that gal back thar?"

"Do you mean the light one or the dark one?"

"You know damn good and well which one I mean," said Jim.

"Yes, I seed her—what about her?" I said.

"Well, nothin'—only I'm a-goin' to marry her," he said.

I knowed then that she had him hooked. And yet I never believed at first that hit would last. Fer Jim had had so many gals—I'd never had a gal in my whole life up to that time, but Lord! Jim would have him a new gal every other week. We had some fine-lookin' fellers in our company, but Jim Weaver was the handsomest feller that you ever seed. He was tall and lean and built just right, and he carried himself as straight as a rod: he had black hair and coal-black eyes, and when he looked at you he could burn a hole through you. And I reckon he'd burned a hole right through the heart of many a gal before he first saw Martha Patton. He could have had his pick of the whole lot—a born lady-killer if you ever seed one—and that was why I never thought that hit'd last.

And maybe hit was a pity that hit did. Fer Jim Weaver until the day that he met Martha Patton had been the most happy-go-lucky feller that you ever seed. He didn't have a care in the whole world—full of fun—ready fer anything and into every kind of devilment and foolishness. But from that moment on he was a different man. And I've always thought that maybe hit was a pity that hit hit him when hit did—that hit had to come jest at that time. If hit had only come a few years later—if hit could only have waited till the war was over! He'd wanted to go so much—he'd looked at the whole thing as a big lark—but now! Well she had him, and he had her: the day they marched us out of town he had her promise, and in his watch he had her picture and a little lock of her black hair, and as they marched us out, and him beside me, we passed her, and she looked at him, and I felt him jerk again and knowed the look she gave him had gone through him like a knife.

From that time on he was a different man; from that time on he was like a man in hell. Hit's funny how hit all turns out—how none of hit is like what we expect. Hit's funny how war and a little black-haired gal will change a man—but that's the story that I'm goin' to tell you now.

The nearest rail head in those days was eighty mile away at Locust Gap. They marched us out of town right up the Fairfield Road along the river up past Crestville, and right across the Blue Ridge there, and down the mountain. We made Old Stockade the first day's march and camped thar fer the night. Hit was twenty-four miles of marchin' right across the mountain, with the roads the way they was in those days, too. And let me tell you, fer new men with only two months' trainin' that was doin' good.

We made Locust Gap in three days and a half, and I wish you'd seed the welcome that they gave us! People were hollerin' and shoutin' the whole way. All the women folk and childern were lined up along the road, bands a-playin', boys runnin' along beside us, good shoes, new uniforms, the finest-lookin' set of fellers that you ever seed—Lord! You'd a-thought we was goin' to a picnic from the way hit looked. And I reckon that was the way most of us felt about hit, too. We thought we was goin' off to have a lot of fun. If anyone had knowed what he was in fer or could a-seed the passel o' scarecrows that came limpin' back barefoot and half naked four years later, I reckon he'd a-thought twice before he 'listed up.

Lord, when I think of hit! When I try to tell about hit thar jest ain't words enough tell what hit was like. And when I think of the way I was when I joined up— and the way I was when I came back four years later! When I went away I was an ignorant country boy, so tenderhearted that I wouldn't harm a rabbit. And when I came back after the war was over I could a-stood by and seed a man murdered right before my eyes with no more feelin' than I'd have had fer a stuck hog. I had no more feelin' about human life than I had fer the life of a sparrer. I'd seed a ten-acre field so thick with dead men that you could have walked all over hit without steppin' on the ground a single time.

And that was where I made my big mistake. If I'd only knowed a little more, if I'd only waited jest a little longer after I got home, things would have been all right. That's been the big regret of my whole life. I never had no education. I never had a chance to git one before I went away. And when I came back I could a-had my schoolin' but I didn't take hit. The reason was I never knowed no better: I'd seed so much fightin' and killin' that I didn't care fer nothin'. I jest felt dead and numb like all the brains had been shot out of me. I jest wanted to git me a little patch of land somewheres and settle down and fergit about the world.

That's where I made my big mistake. I didn't wait long enough. I got married too soon, and after that the childern came and hit was root, hawg, or die: I had to grub fer hit. But if I'd only waited jest a little while hit would have been all right. In less'n a year hit all cleared up. I got my health back, pulled myself together and got my feet back on the ground, and had more mercy and understandin' in me, jest on account of all the sufferin' I'd seen, than I ever had. And as fer my head, why hit was better than hit ever was: with all I'd seen and knowed I could a-got a schoolin' in no time. But you see I wouldn't wait. I didn't think that hit'd ever come back. I was jest sick of livin'.

But as I say—they marched us down to Locust Gap in less'n four days' time, and then they put us on the cars fer Richmond. We got to Richmond on the mornin' of one day, and up to that very moment we had thought that they was sendin' us to join Lee's army in the north. But the next mornin' we got our orders—and they was sendin' us out west. They had been fightin' in Kentucky: we was in trouble thar; they sent us out to stop the Army of the Cumberland. And that was the last I ever saw of old Virginny. From that time on we fought it out thar in the west and south. That's where we war, the Twenty-ninth, from then on to the end.

We had no real big fights until the spring of '62. And hit takes a fight to make a soldier of a man. Before that, thar was skirmishin' and raids in Tennessee and in Kentucky. That winter we seed hard marchin' in the cold and wind and rain. We learned to know what hunger was, and what hit was to have to draw your belly in to fit your rations. I reckon by that time we knowed hit wasn't goin' to be a picnic like we thought that hit would be. We was a-learnin' all the time, but we wasn't soldiers yet. It takes a good big fight to make a soldier, and we hadn't had one yet. Early in '62 we almost had one. They marched us to the relief of Donelson—but law! They had taken her before we got thar—and I'm goin' to tell you a good story about that.

U. S. Grant was thar to take her, and we was marchin' to relieve her before old Butcher could git in. We was seven mile away, and hit was comin' on to sundown—we'd been marchin' hard. We got the order to fall out and rest. And that was when I heared the gun and knowed that Donelson had fallen. Thar was no sound of fightin'. Everything was still as Sunday. We was sittin' thar aside the road and then I heared a cannon boom. Hit boomed five times, real slow like—Boom!—Boom!—Boom!—Boom!—Boom! And the moment that I heared hit, I had a premonition. I turned to Jim and I said: "Well, thar you are! That's Donelson—and she's surrendered!"

Cap'n Bob Saunders heared me, but he wouldn't believe me and he said: "You're wrong!"

"Well," said Jim, "I hope to God he's right. I wouldn't care if the whole damn war had fallen through. I'm ready to go home."

"Well, he's wrong," said Captain Bob, "and I'll bet money on hit that he is."

Well, I tell you, that jest suited me. That was the way I was in those days—right from the beginnin' of the war to the very end. If thar was any fun or devil-ment goin' on, any card playin' or gamblin', or any other kind of foolishness, I was right in on hit. I'd a-bet a man that red was green or that day was night, and if a gal had looked at me from a persimmon tree, why, law! I reckon I'd a-clumb the tree to git her. That's jest the way hit was with me all through the war. I never made a bet or played a game of cards in my life before the war or after hit was over, but while the war was goin' on I was ready fer anything.

"How much will you bet?" I said.

"I'll bet you a hundred dollars even money," said Bob Saunders, and no sooner got the words out of his mouth than the bet was on.

We planked the money down right thar and gave hit to Jim to hold the stakes. Well, sir, we didn't have to wait half an hour before a feller on a horse came ridin' up and told us hit was no use goin' any farther—Fort Donelson had fallen.

"What did I tell you?" I said to Cap'n Saunders, and I put the money in my pocket.

Well, the laugh was on him then. I wish you could a-seen the expression on his face—he looked mighty sheepish, I tell you. But he admitted hit, you know, he had to own up.

"You were right," he said. "You won the bet. But—

I'll tell you what I'll do!" He put his hand into his pocket and pulled out a roll of bills. "I've got a hundred dollars left—and with me hit's all or nothin'! We'll draw cards fer this last hundred, mine against yorn—high card wins!"

Well, I was ready fer him. I pulled out my hundred, and I said, "Git out the deck!"

So they brought the deck out then and Jim Weaver shuffled hit and held hit while we drew. Bob Saunders drawed first and he drawed the eight of spades. When I turned my card up I had one of the queens.

Well, sir, you should have seen the look upon Bob Saunders' face. I tell you what, the fellers whooped and hollered till he looked like he was ready to crawl through a hole in the floor. We all had some fun with him, and then, of course, I gave the money back. I never kept a penny in my life I made from gamblin'.

But that's the way hit was with me in those days—I was ready fer hit—fer anything. If any kind of devilment or foolishness came up I was right in on hit with the ringleaders.

Well then, Fort Donelson was the funniest fight that I was ever in because hit was all fun fer me without no fightin'. And that jest suited me. And Stone Mountain was the most peculiar fight that I was in because—well, I'll tell you a strange story and you can figger fer yourself if you ever heared about a fight like that before.

Did you ever hear of a battle in which one side never fired a shot and yet won the fight and did more damage and more destruction to the other side than all the guns and cannon in the world could do? Well, that was the battle of Stone Mountain. Now, I was in a lot of battles. But the battle of Stone Mountain was the queerest one of the whole war.

I'll tell you how hit was.

We was up on top of the Mountain and the Yankees was below us tryin' to drive us out and take the Mountain. We couldn't git our guns up thar, we didn't try to —we didn't have to git our guns up thar. The only gun I ever seed up thar was a little brass howitzer that we pulled up with ropes, but we never fired a shot with hit. We didn't git a chance to use hit. We no more'n got hit in position before a shell exploded right on top of hit and split that little howitzer plumb in two. Hit jest fell into two parts: you couldn't have made a neater job of hit if you'd cut hit down the middle with a saw. I'll never fergit that little howitzer and the way they split hit plumb in two.

As for the rest of the fightin' on our side, hit was done with rocks and stones. We gathered together a great pile of rocks and stones and boulders all along the top of the Mountain, and when they attacked we waited and let 'em have hit.

The Yankees attacked in three lines, one after the other. We waited until the first line was no more'n thirty feet below us—until we could see the whites of their eyes, as the sayin' goes—and then we let 'em have hit. We jest rolled those boulders down on 'em, and I tell you what, hit was an awful thing to watch. I never saw no worse destruction than that with guns and cannon during the whole war.

You could hear 'em screamin' and hollerin' until hit made your blood run cold. They kept comin' on and we mowed 'em down by the hundreds. We mowed 'em down without firin' a single shot. We crushed them, wiped them out—jest by rollin' those big rocks and boulders down on them.

There was bigger battles in the war, but Stone Mountain was the queerest one I ever seed.

* * *

Fort Donelson came early in the war, and Stone Mountain came later toward the end. And one was funny and the other was peculiar, but thar was fightin' in between that wasn't neither one. I'm goin' to tell you about that.

Fort Donelson was the first big fight that we was in —and as I say, we wasn't really in hit because we couldn't git to her in time. And after Donelson that spring, in April, thar was Shiloh. Well—all that I can tell you is, we was thar on time at Shiloh. Oh Lord, I reckon that we was! Perhaps we had been country boys before, perhaps some of us still made a joke of hit before—but after Shiloh we wasn't country boys no longer. We didn't make a joke about hit after Shiloh. They wiped the smile off of our faces at Shiloh. And after Shiloh we was boys no longer: we was vet'ran men.

From then on hit was fightin' to the end. That's where we learned what hit was like—at Shiloh. From then on we knowed what hit would be until the end.

Jim got wounded thar at Shiloh. Hit wasn't bad— not bad enough to suit him anyways—fer he wanted to go home fer good. Hit was a flesh wound in the leg, but hit was some time before they could git to him, and he was layin' out thar on the field and I reckon that he lost some blood. Anyways, he was unconscious when they picked him up. They carried him back and dressed his wound right thar upon the field. They cleaned hit out, I reckon, and they bandaged hit—thar was so many of 'em they couldn't do much more than that. Oh, I tell you what, in those days thar wasn't much that they could do. I've seed the surgeons workin' underneath an open shed with meatsaws, choppin' off the arms and legs and throwin' 'em out thar in a pile like they was sticks of wood, sometimes without no chloroform or nothin', and the screamin' and the hollerin' of the men was enough to make your head turn gray. And that was as much as anyone could do. Hit was live or die and take your chance—and thar was so many of 'em wounded so much worse than Jim that I reckon he was lucky they did anything fer him at all.

I heared 'em tell about hit later, how he came to, a-lyin' stretched out thar on an old dirty blanket on the bare floor, and an army surgeon seed him lookin' at his leg all bandaged up and I reckon thought he'd cheer him up and said: "Oh, that ain't nothin'—you'll be up and fightin' Yanks again in two weeks' time."

Well, with that, they said, Jim got to cursin' and a-takin' on something terrible. They said the language he used was enough to make your hair stand up on end. They said he screamed and raved and reached down thar and jerked that bandage off and said—"Like hell I will!" They said the blood spouted up thar like a fountain, and they said that army doctor was so mad he throwed Jim down upon his back and sat on him and he took that bandage, all bloody as hit was, and he tied hit back around his leg again and he said: "Goddam you, if you pull that bandage off again, I'll let you bleed to death."

And Jim, they said, came ragin' back at him until you could have heared him fer a mile, and said: "Well, by God, I don't care if I do; I'd rather die than stay here any longer."

They say they had hit back and forth thar until Jim got so weak he couldn't talk no more. I know that when I come to see him a day or two later he was settin' up and I asked him: "Jim, how is your leg? Are you hurt bad?"

And he answered: "Not bad enough. They can take the whole damn leg off," he said, "as far as I'm con-

cerned, and bury hit here at Shiloh if they'll only let me
go back home and not come back again. Me and Martha
will git along somehow," he said. "I'd rather be a crip-
ple the rest of my life than have to come back and fight
in this damn war."

Well, I knowed he meant hit too. I looked at him
and seed how much he meant hit, and I knowed thar
wasn't anything that I could do. When a man begins to
talk that way, thar hain't much you can say to him.
Well, sure enough, in a week or two, they let him go
upon a two months' furlough and he went limpin' away
upon a crutch. He was the happiest man I ever seed.
"They gave me two months' leave," he said, "but if
they jest let me git back home old Bragg'll have to send
his whole damn army before he gits me out of thar
again."

Well, he was gone two months or more, and I never
knowed what happened—whether he got ashamed of
himself when his wound healed up all right, or whether
Martha talked him out of hit. But he was back with us
again by late July—the grimmest, bitterest-lookin' man
you ever seed. He wouldn't talk to me about hit, he
wouldn't tell me what had happened, but I knowed
from that time on he'd never draw his breath in peace
until he left the army and got back home fer good.

Well, that was Shiloh, that was the time we didn't
miss, that was where we lost our grin, where we
knowed at last what hit would be until the end.

I've told you of three battles now, and one was
funny, one was strange, and one was—well, one
showed us what war and fightin' could be like. But I'll
tell you of a fourth one now. And the fourth one was
the greatest of the lot.

We seed some big fights in the war. And we was in
some bloody battles. But the biggest fight we fought

was Chickamauga. The bloodiest fight I ever seed was Chickamauga. Thar was big battles in the war, but thar never was a fight before, thar'll never be a fight again, like Chickamauga. I'm goin' to tell you how hit was at Chickamauga.

All through the spring and summer of that year Old Rosey follered us through Tennessee.

We had him stopped the year before, the time we whupped him at Stone's River at the end of '62. We tard him out so bad he had to wait. He waited thar six months at Murfreesboro. But we knowed he was a-comin' all the time. Old Rosey started at the end of June and drove us out to Shelbyville. We fell back on Tullahoma in rains the like of which you never seed. The rains that fell the last week in June that year was terrible. But Rosey kept a-comin' on.

He drove us out of Tullahoma too. We fell back across the Cumberland, we pulled back behind the mountain, but he follered us.

I reckon thar was fellers that was quicker when a fight was on, and when they'd seed just what hit was they had to do. But when it came to plannin' and a-figgerin', Old Rosey Rosecrans took the cake. Old Rosey was a fox. Fer sheer natural cunnin' I never knowed the beat of him.

While Bragg was watchin' him at Chattanooga to keep him from gittin' across the Tennessee, he sent some fellers forty mile up stream. And then he'd march 'em back and forth and round the hill and back in front of us again where we could look at 'em, until you'd a-thought that every Yankee in the world was there. But laws! All that was just a dodge! He had fellers a-sawin't and a-hammerin', a-buildin' boats, a-blowin' bugles and a-beatin' drums, makin' all the noise they could—you could hear 'em over yonder gittin' ready—and all the time Old Rosey was fifty mile or more down stream, ten mile past Chattanooga, a-fixin' to git over way down thar. That was the kind of feller Rosey was.

We reached Chattanooga early in July and waited fer two months. Old Rosey hadn't caught up with us yet. He still had to cross the Cumberland, push his men and pull his trains across the ridges and through the gaps before he got to us. July went by, we had no news of him. "Oh Lord!" said Jim, "perhaps he ain't a-comin!" I knowed he was a-comin', but I let Jim have his way.

Some of the fellers would git used to hit. A feller'd git into a frame of mind where he wouldn't let hit worry him. He'd let termorrer look out fer hitself. That was the way hit was with me.

With Jim hit was the other way around. Now that he knowed Martha Patton he was a different man. I think he hated the war and army life from the moment that he met her. From that time he was livin' only fer one thing—to go back home and marry that gal. When mail would come and some of us was gittin' letters he'd be the first in line; and if she wrote him why he'd walk away like someone in a dream. And if she failed to write he'd jest go off somers and set down by himself: he'd be in such a state of misery he didn't want to talk to no one. He got the reputation with the fellers fer bein' queer—unsociable—always a-broodin' and a-frettin' about somethin' and a-wantin' to be left alone. And so, after a time, they let him be. He wasn't popular with most of them—but they never knowed what was wrong, they never knowed that he wasn't really the way they thought he was at all. Hit was jest that he was hit so desperate hard, the worst-in-love man that I ever seed. But law! I knowed what was the trouble from the start.

Hit's funny how war took a feller. Before the war I was the serious one, and Jim had been the one to play.

I reckon that I'd had to work too hard. We was so poor. Before the war hit almost seemed I never knowed the time I didn't have to work. And when the war came, why I only thought of all the fun and frolic I was goin' to have; and then at last, when I knowed what hit was like, why I was used to hit and didn't care.

I always could git used to things. And I reckon maybe that's the reason that I'm here. I wasn't one to worry much, and no matter how rough the goin' got I always figgered I could hold out if the others could. I let termorrer look out fer hitself. I reckon that you'd have to say I was an optimist. If things got bad, well, I always figgered that they could be worse; and if they got so bad they couldn't be no worse, why then I'd figger that they couldn't last this way ferever, they'd have to git some better sometime later on.

I reckon toward the end thar, when they got so bad we didn't think they'd ever git no better, I'd reached the place where I jest didn't care. I could still lay down and go to sleep and not worry over what was goin' to come termorrer, because I never knowed what was to come and so I didn't let hit worry me. I reckon you'd have to say that was the Pentland in me—our belief in what we call predestination.

Now, Jim was jest the other way. Before the war he was happy as a lark and thought of nothin' except havin' fun. But then the war came and hit changed him so you wouldn't a-knowed he was the same man.

And, as I say, hit didn't happen all at once. Jim was the happiest man I ever seed that mornin' that we started out from home. I reckon he thought of the war as we all did, as a big frolic. We gave hit jest about six months. We figgered we'd be back by then, and of course all that jest suited Jim. I reckon that suited all of us. It would give us all a chance to wear a uniform and to see the world, to shoot some Yankees and to run 'em north, and then to come back home and lord it over those who hadn't been and be a hero and court the gals.

That was the way hit looked to us when we set out from Zebulon. We never thought about the winter. We never thought about the mud and cold and rain. We never knowed what hit would be to have to march on an empty belly, to have to march barefoot with frozen feet and with no coat upon your back, to have to lay down on bare ground and try to sleep with no coverin' above you, and thankful half the time if you could find dry ground to sleep upon, and too tard the rest of hit to care. We never knowed or thought about such things as these. We never knowed how hit would be there in the cedar thickets beside Chickamauga Creek. And if we had a-knowed, if someone had a-told us, why I reckon that none of us would a-cared. We was too young and ignorant to care. And as fer knowin't—law! The only trouble about knowin' is that you've got to know what knowin's like before you know what knowin' is. Thar's no one that can tell you. You've got to know hit fer yourself.

Well, like I say, we'd been fightin' all this time and still thar was no sign of the war endin'. Old Rosey jest kept a-follerin' us and—"Lord!" Jim would say, "will it never end?"

I never knowed myself. We'd been fightin' fer two years, and I'd given over knowin' long ago. With Jim hit was different. He'd been a-prayin' and a-hopin' from the first that soon hit would be over and that he could go back and get that gal. And at first, fer a year or more, I tried to cheer him up. I told him that it couldn't last forever. But after a while hit wasn't no use to tell him that. He wouldn't believe me any longer.

Because Old Rosey kept a-comin' on. We'd whup him and we'd stop him fer a while, but then he'd git his wind, he'd be on our trail again, he'd drive us back.— "Oh Lord!" said Jim, "will hit never stop?"

That summer I been tellin' you about, he drove us down through Tennessee. He drove us out of Shelbyville, and we fell back on Tullahoma, to the passes of the hills. When we pulled back across the Cumberland I said to Jim: "Now we've got him. He'll have to cross the mountains now to git at us. And when he does, we'll have him. That's all that Bragg's been waitin' fer. We'll whup the daylights out of him this time," I said, "and after that thar'll be nothin' left of him. We'll be home by Christmas, Jim—you wait and see."

And Jim just looked at me and shook his head and said: "Lord, Lord, I don't believe this war'll ever end!"

Hit wasn't that he was afraid—or, if he was, hit made a wildcat of him in the fightin'. Jim could get fightin' mad like no one else I ever seed. He could do things, take chances no one else I ever knowed would take. But I reckon hit was jest because he was so desperate. He hated hit so much. He couldn't git used to hit the way the others could. He couldn't take hit as hit came. Hit wasn't so much that he was afraid to die. I guess hit was that he was still so full of livin'. He didn't want to die because he wanted to live so much. And he wanted to live so much because he was in love.

. . . So, like I say, Old Rosey finally pushed us back across the Cumberland. He was in Chattanooga in July, and fer a few weeks hit was quiet thar. But all the time I knowed that Rosey would keep comin' on. We got wind of him again along in August. He had started after us again. He pushed his trains across the Cumberland, with the roads so bad, what with the rains, his wagons sunk down to the axle hubs. But he got 'em over, came down in the valley, then across the ridge, and early in September he was on our heels again.

We cleared out of Chattanooga on the eighth. And our tail end was pullin' out at one end of the town as Rosey came in through the other. We dropped down around the mountain south of town and Rosey thought he had us on the run again.

But this time he was fooled. We was ready fer him now, a-pickin' out our spot and layin' low. Old Rosey follered us. He sent McCook around down toward the south to head us off. He thought he had us in retreat but when McCook got thar we wasn't thar at all. We'd come down south of town and taken our positions along Chickamauga Creek. McCook had gone too far. Thomas was follerin' us from the north and when McCook tried to git back to join Thomas, he couldn't pass us, fer we blocked the way. They had to fight us or be cut in two.

We was in position on the Chickamauga on the seventeenth. The Yankees streamed in on the eighteenth, and took their position in the woods a-facin' us. We had our backs to Lookout Mountain and the Chickamauga Creek. The Yankees had their line thar in the woods before us on a rise, with Missionary Ridge behind them to the east.

The Battle of Chickamauga was fought in a cedar thicket. That cedar thicket, from what I knowed of hit, was about three miles long and one mile wide. We fought fer two days all up and down that thicket and to and fro across hit. When the fight started that cedar thicket was so thick and dense you could a-took a butcher knife and drove hit in thar anywheres and hit would a-stuck. And when that fight was over that cedar thicket had been so destroyed by shot and shell you could a-looked in thar anywheres with your naked eye and seed a black snake run a hundred yards away. If you'd a-looked at that cedar thicket the day after that fight was over you'd a-wondered how a hummin' bird the size of your thumb-nail could a-flown through thar without bein' torn into pieces by the fire. And yet more than half of us who went into that thicket came out of hit alive and told the tale. You wouldn't have thought that hit was possible. But I was thar and seed hit, and hit was.

A little after midnight—hit may have been about two o'clock that mornin', while we lay there waitin' for the fight we knowed was bound to come next day—Jim woke me up. I woke up like a flash—you got used to hit in those days—and though hit was so dark you could hardly see your hand a foot away, I knowed his face at once. He was white as a ghost and he had got thin as a rail in that last year's campaign. In the dark his face looked white as paper. He dug his hand into my arm so hard hit hurt. I roused up sharp-like; then I seed him and knowed who hit was.

"John!" he said—"John!"—and he dug his fingers in my arm so hard he made hit ache—"John! I've seed him! He was here again!"

I tell you what, the way he said hit made my blood run cold. They say we Pentlands are a superstitious people, and perhaps we are. They told hit how they saw my brother George a-comin' up the hill one day at sunset, how they all went out upon the porch and waited fer him, how everyone, the children and the grown-ups alike, all seed him as he clumb the hill, and how he passed behind a tree and disappeared as if the ground had swallered him—and how they got the news ten days later that he'd been killed at Chancellorsville on that very day and hour. I've heared these stories and I know the others all believe them, but I never put no stock in them myself. And yet, I tell you what! The sight of that white face and those black eyes a-burnin' at me in the dark—the way he said hit and the way hit was—fer I could feel the men around me and hear somethin' movin' in the wood—I heared a trace chain rattle and hit was enough to make your blood run cold! I grabbed hold of him—I shook him by the arm—I didn't want the rest of 'em to hear—I told him to hush up—

"John, he was here!" he said.

I never asked him what he meant—I knowed too well to ask. It was the third time he'd seed hit in a month—a man upon a horse. I didn't want to hear no more—I told him that hit was a dream and I told him to go back to sleep.

"I tell you, John, hit was no dream!" he said. "Oh John, I heared hit—and I heared his horse—and I seed him sittin' thar as plain as day—and he never said a word to me—he jest sat thar lookin' down, and then he turned and rode away into the woods. . . . John, John, I heared him and I don't know what hit means!"

Well, whether he seed hit or imagined hit or dreamed hit, I don't know. But the sight of his black eyes a-burnin' holes through me in the dark made me feel almost as if I'd seed hit, too. I told him to lay down by me—and still I seed his eyes a-blazin' thar. I know he didn't sleep a wink the rest of that whole night. I closed my eyes and tried to make him think that I was sleepin' but hit was no use—we lay thar wide awake. And both of us was glad when mornin' came.

The fight began upon our right at ten o'clock. We couldn't find out what was happenin': the woods thar was so close and thick we never knowed fer two days what had happened, and we didn't know fer certain then. We never knowed how many we was fightin' or how many we had lost. I've heared them say that even Old Rosey himself didn't know jest what had happened when he rode back into town next day, and didn't know that Thomas was still standin' like a rock. And if Old Rosey didn't know no more than this about hit, what could a common soldier know? We fought back and forth across that cedar thicket for two days, and thar was times when you would be right up on top of them before you even knowed that they was thar. And that's the way the fightin' went—the bloodiest fightin' that was ever knowed, until that cedar thicket was soaked red with blood, and thar was hardly a place left in thar where a sparrer could have perched.

And as I say, we heared 'em fightin' out upon our right at ten o'clock, and then the fightin' came our way. I heared later that this fightin' started when the Yanks come down to the Creek and run into a bunch of Forrest's men and drove 'em back. And then they had hit back and forth until they got drove back themselves, and that's the way we had hit all day long. We'd attack and then they'd throw us back, then they'd attack and we'd beat them off. And that was the way hit went from mornin' till night. We piled up there upon their left: they mowed us down with canister and grape until the very grass was soakin' with our blood, but we kept comin' on. We must have charged a dozen times that day—I was in four of 'em myself. We fought back and forth across that wood until there wasn't a piece of hit as big as the palm of your hand we hadn't fought on. We busted through their right at two-thirty in the afternoon and got way over past the Widder Glenn's, where Rosey had his quarters, and beat 'em back until we got the whole way 'cross the Lafayette Road and took possession of the road. And then they drove us out again.

And we kept comin' on, and both sides were still at hit after darkness fell.

We fought back and forth across that road all day with first one side and then the t'other holdin' hit until that road hitself was soaked in blood. They called that road the Bloody Lane, and that was jest the name fer hit.

We kept fightin' an hour or more after hit had gotten dark, and you could see the rifles flashin' in the woods, but then hit all died down. I tell you what, that night was somethin' to remember and to marvel at as long as you live. The fight had set the wood afire in places, and you could see the smoke and flames and hear the screamin' and the hollerin' of the wounded until hit made your blood run cold. We got as many as we could—but some we didn't even try to git—we jest let 'em lay. It was an awful thing to hear. I reckon many a wounded man was jest left to die or burn to death because we couldn't git 'em out.

You could see the nurses and the stretcher-bearers movin' through the woods, and each side huntin' fer hits dead. You could see them movin' in the smoke an' flames, an' you could see the dead men layin' there as thick as wheat, with their corpse-like faces 'n black powder on their lips, an' a little bit of moonlight comin' through the trees, and all of hit more like a nightmare out of hell than anything I ever knowed before.

But we had other work to do. All through the night we could hear the Yanks a-choppin' and a-thrashin' round, and we knowed that they was fellin' trees to block us when we went fer them next mornin'. Fer we knowed the fight was only jest begun. We figgered that we'd had the best of hit, but we knowed no one had won the battle yet. We knowed the second day would beat the first.

Jim knowed hit too. Poor Jim, he didn't sleep that night—he never seed the man upon the horse that night he jest sat there, a-grippin' his knees and starin', and a-sayin'; "Lord God, Lord God, when will hit ever end?"

Then mornin' came at last. This time we knowed jest where we was and what hit was we had to do. Our line was fixed by that time. Bragg knowed at last where Rosey had his line, and Rosey knowed where we was. So we waited there, both sides, till mornin' came. Hit was a foggy mornin' with mist upon the ground. Around ten o'clock when the mist began to rise, we got the order and we went chargin' through the wood again.

We knowed the fight was goin' to be upon the right —upon our right, that is—on Rosey's left. And we knowed that Thomas was in charge on Rosey's left. And we all knowed that hit was easier to crack a flint rock with your teeth than to make old Thomas budge. But we went after him, and I tell you what, that was a fight! The first day's fight had been like playin' marbles when compared to this.

We hit old Thomas on his left at half-past ten, and Breckenridge came sweepin' round and turned old Thomas's flank and came in at his back, and then we had hit hot and heavy. Old Thomas whupped his men around like he would crack a raw-hide whup and drove Breckenridge back around the flank again, but we was back on top of him before you knowed the first attack was over.

The fight went ragin' down the flank, down to the center of Old Rosey's army and back and forth across the left, and all up and down old Thomas's line. We'd hit him right and left and in the middle, and he'd come back at us and throw us back again. And we went

ragin' back and forth thar like two bloody lions with
that cedar thicket so tore up, so bloody and so thick
with dead by that time, that hit looked as if all hell had
broken loose in thar.

Rosey kept a-whuppin' men around off of his right,
to help old Thomas on the left to stave us off. And then
we'd hit old Thomas left of center and we'd bang him
in the middle and we'd hit him on his left again, and
he'd whup those Yankees back and forth off of the right
into his flanks and middle as we went fer him, until we
run those Yankees ragged. We had them gallopin' back
and forth like kangaroos, and in the end that was the
thing that cooked their goose.

The worst fightin' had been on the left, on
Thomas's line, but to hold us thar they'd thinned their
right out and had failed to close in on the center of their
line. And at two o'clock that afternoon when Longstreet
seed the gap in Wood's position on the right, he took
five brigades of us and poured us through. That
whupped them. That broke their line and smashed their
whole right all to smithereens. We went after them like
a pack of ragin' devils. We killed 'em and we took 'em
by the thousands, and those we didn't kill and take
right thar went streamin' back across the Ridge as if all
hell was at their heels.

That was a rout if ever I heared tell of one! They
went streamin' back across the Ridge—hit was each
man fer himself and the devil take the hindmost. They
caught Rosey comin' up—he rode into them—he tried
to check 'em, face 'em round, and get 'em to come on
again—hit was like tryin' to swim the Mississippi up-
stream on a boneyard mule! They swept him back with
them as if he'd been a wooden chip. They went
streamin' into Rossville like the rag-tag of creation—the

worst whupped army that you ever seed, and Old Rosey was along with all the rest!

He knowed hit was all up with him, or thought he knowed hit, for everybody told him the Army of the Cumberland had been blowed to smithereens and that hit was a general rout. And Old Rosey turned and rode to Chattanooga, and he was a beaten man. I've heared tell that when he rode up to his headquarters thar in Chattanooga they had to help him from his horse, and that he walked into the house all dazed and fuddled-like, like he never knowed what had happened to him— and that he jest sat thar struck dumb and never spoke.

This was at four o'clock of that same afternoon. And then the news was brought to him that Thomas was still thar upon the field and wouldn't budge. Old Thomas stayed thar like a rock. We'd smashed the right, we'd sent it flyin' back across the Ridge, the whole Yankee right was broken into bits and streamin' back to Rossville for dear life. Then we bent old Thomas back upon his left. We thought we had him, he'd have to leave the field or else surrender. But old Thomas turned and fell back along the Ridge and put his back against the wall thar, and he wouldn't budge.

Longstreet pulled us back at three o'clock when we had broken up the right and sent them streamin' back across the Ridge. We thought that hit was over then. We moved back stumblin' like men walkin' in a dream. And I turned to Jim—I put my arm around him, and I said: "Jim, what did I say? I knowed hit, we've licked 'em and this is the end!" I never even knowed if he heard me. He went stumblin' on beside me with his face as white as paper and his lips black with the powder of the cartridge-bite, mumblin' and mutterin' to himself like someone talkin' in a dream. And we fell back to position, and they told us all to rest. And we leaned thar on our rifles like men who hardly knowed if they had come out of that hell alive or dead.

"Oh Jim, we've got 'em and this is the end!" I said.

He leaned thar swayin' on his rifle, starin' through the wood. He jest leaned and swayed thar, and he never said a word, and those great eyes of his a-burnin' through the wood.

"Jim, don't you hear me?"—and I shook him by the arm. "Hit's over, man! We've licked 'em and the fight is over!—Can't you understand?"

And then I heared them shoutin' on the right, the word came down the line again, and Jim—poor Jim!— he raised his head and listened, and "Oh God!" he said, "we've got to go again!"

Well, hit was true. The word had come that Thomas had lined up upon the Ridge, and we had to go fer him again. After that I never exactly knowed what happened. Hit was like fightin' in a bloody dream—like doin' somethin' in a nightmare—only the nightmare was like death and hell. Longstreet threw us up that hill five times, I think, before darkness came. We'd charge up to the very muzzles of their guns, and they'd mow us down like grass, and we'd come stumblin' back—or what was left of us—and form again at the foot of the hill, and then come on again. We'd charge right up the Ridge and drive 'em through the gap and fight 'em with cold steel, and they'd come back again and we'd brain each other with the butt end of our guns. Then they'd throw us back and we'd re-form and come on after 'em again.

The last charge happened jest at dark. We came along and stripped the ammunition off the dead—we took hit from the wounded—we had nothin' left ourselves. Then we hit the first line—and we drove them back. We hit the second and swept over them. We were goin' up to take the third and last—they waited till they saw the color of our eyes before they let us have hit. Hit was like a river of red-hot lead had poured down on us: the line melted thar like snow. Jim stumbled and spun round as if somethin' had whupped him like a top. He fell right toward me, with his eyes wide open and the blood a-pourin' from his mouth. I took one look at him and then stepped over him like he was a log. Thar was no more to see or think of now—no more to reach— except that line. We reached hit and they let us have hit —and we stumbled back.

And yet we knowed that we had won a victory. That's what they told us later—and we knowed hit must be so because when daybreak came next mornin' the Yankees was all gone. They had all retreated into town, and we was left there by the Creek at Chicka-mauga in possession of the field.

I don't know how many men got killed. I don't know which side lost the most. I only know you could have walked across the dead men without settin' foot upon the ground. I only know that cedar thicket which had been so dense and thick two days before you could've drove a knife into hit and hit would of stuck, had been so shot to pieces that you could've looked in thar on Monday mornin' with your naked eye and seed a black snake run a hundred yards away.

I don't know how many men we lost or how many of the Yankees we may have killed. The Generals on both sides can figger all that out to suit themselves. But I know that when that fight was over you could have looked in thar and wondered how a hummin' bird could've flown through that cedar thicket and come out alive. And yet that happened, yes, and something more than hummin' birds—fer men came out, alive.

And on that Monday mornin', when I went back

up the Ridge to where Jim lay, thar just beside him on a little torn piece of bough, I heard a redbird sing. I turned Jim over and got his watch, his pocket-knife, and what few papers and belongin's that he had, and some letters that he'd had from Martha Patton. And I put them in my pocket.

And then I got up and looked around. It all seemed funny after hit had happened, like something that had happened in a dream. Fer Jim had wanted so desperate hard to live, and hit had never mattered half so much to me, and now I was a-standin' thar with Jim's watch and Martha Patton's letters in my pocket and a-listenin' to that little redbird sing.

And I would go all through the war and go back home and marry Martha later on, and fellers like poor Jim was layin' thar at Chickamauga Creek.

Hit's all so strange now when you think of hit. Hit all turned out so different from the way we thought. And that was long ago, and I'll be ninety-five years old if I am livin' on the seventh day of August, of this present year. Now that's goin' back a long ways, hain't hit? And yet hit all comes back to me as clear as if hit happened yesterday. And then hit all will go away and be as strange as if hit happened in a dream.

But I have been in some big battles I can tell you. I've seen strange things and been in bloody fights. But the biggest fight that I was ever in—the bloodiest battle anyone has ever fought—was at Chickamauga in that cedar thicket—at Chickamauga Creek in that great war.

An Occurrence at Owl Creek Bridge

AMBROSE BIERCE

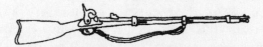

A man stood upon a railroad bridge in northern Alabama, looking down into the swift water twenty feet below. The man's hands were behind his back, the wrists bound with a cord. A rope closely encircled his neck. It was attached to a stout cross-timber above his head and the slack fell to the level of his knees. Some loose boards laid upon the sleepers supporting the metals of the railway supplied a footing for him and his executioners—two private soldiers of the Federal army, directed by a sergeant who in civil life may have been a deputy sheriff. At a short remove upon the same temporary platform was an officer in the uniform of his rank, armed. He was a captain. A sentinel at each end of the bridge stood with his rifle in the position known as "support," that is to say, vertical in front of the left shoulder, the hammer resting on the forearm thrown straight across the chest—a formal and unnatural position, enforcing an erect carriage of the body. It did not appear to be the duty of these two men to know what was occurring at the centre of the bridge; they merely blockaded the two ends of the foot planking that traversed it.

Beyond one of the sentinels nobody was in sight; the railroad ran straight away into a forest for a hundred yards, then, curving, was lost to view. Doubtless there was an outpost farther along. The other bank of the stream was open ground—a gentle acclivity topped with a stockade of vertical tree trunks, loop-holed for rifles, with a single embrasure through which protruded the muzzle of a brass cannon commanding the bridge. Midway of the slope between bridge and fort were the spectators—a single company of infantry in line at "parade rest," the butts of the rifles on the ground, the barrels inclining slightly backward against the right shoulder, the hands crossed on the stock. A lieutenant stood at the right of the line, the point of his sword upon the ground, his left hand rested upon his right. Excepting the group of four at the centre of the bridge, not a man moved. The company faced the bridge, staring stonily, motionless. The sentinels, facing the banks of the stream, might have been statues to adorn the bridge. The captain stood with folded arms, silent, observing the work of his subordinates, but making no sign. Death is a dignitary who when he comes announced is to be received with formal manifestations of respect, even by those most familiar with him. In the code of military etiquette silence and fixity are forms of deference.

The man who was engaged in being hanged was apparently about thirty-five years of age. He was a civilian, if one might judge from his habit, which was that of a planter. His features were good—a straight nose, firm mouth, broad forehead, from which his long, dark hair was combed straight back, falling behind his ears to the collar of his well-fitting frock-coat. He wore a mustache and pointed beard, but no whiskers; his eyes were large and dark gray, and had a kindly expression which one would hardly have expected in one whose neck was in the hemp. Evidently this was no vulgar assassin. The liberal military code makes provision for hanging many kinds of persons, and gentlemen are not excluded.

The preparations being complete, the two private soldiers stepped aside and each drew away the plank upon which he had been standing. The sergeant turned to the captain, saluted and placed himself immediately behind that officer, who in turned moved apart one pace. These movements left the condemned man and the sergeant standing on the two ends of the same plank, which spanned three of the cross-ties of the bridge. The end upon which the civilian stood almost, but not quite, reached a fourth. This plank had been held in place by the weight of the captain; it was now held by that of the sergeant. At a signal from the former the latter would step aside, the plank would tilt and the condemned man go down between two ties. The arrangement commended itself to his judgment as simple and effective. His face had not been covered nor his eyes bandaged. He looked a moment at his "unsteadfast footing," then let his gaze wander to the swirling water of the stream racing madly beneath his feet. A piece of dancing driftwood caught his attention and his eyes followed it down the current. How slowly it appeared to move! What a sluggish stream!

He closed his eyes in order to fix his last thoughts upon his wife and children. The water, touched to gold by the early sun, the brooding mists under the banks at some distance down the stream, the fort, the soldiers, the piece of drift—all had distracted him. And now he became conscious of a new disturbance. Striking through the thought of his dear ones was a sound which he could neither ignore nor understand, a sharp, distinct, metallic percussion like the stroke of a blacksmith's hammer upon the anvil; it had the same ringing quality. He wondered what it was and whether immeasurably distant or near by—it seemed both. Its recurrence was regular, but as slow as the tolling of a death knell. He awaited each stroke with impatience and—he knew not why—apprehension. The intervals of silence grew progressively longer; the delays became maddening. With their greater infrequency the sounds increased in strength and sharpness. They hurt his ear like the thrust of a knife; he feared he would shriek. What he heard was the ticking of his watch.

He unclosed his eyes and saw again the water below him. "If I could free my hands," he thought, "I might throw off the noose and spring into the stream. By diving I could evade the bullets and, swimming vigorously, reach the bank, take to the woods and get away home. My home, thank God, is as yet outside their lines; my wife and little ones are still beyond the invader's farthest advance."

As these thoughts, which have here to be set down in words, were flashed into the doomed man's brain rather than evolved from it the captain nodded to the sergeant. The sergeant stepped aside.

2

Peyton Farquhar was a well-to-do planter, of an old and highly respected Alabama family. Being a slave owner and like other slave owners a politician he was naturally an original secessionist and ardently devoted to the Southern cause. Circumstances of an imperious nature, which it is unnecessary to relate here, had prevented him from taking service with the gallant army that had fought the disastrous campaigns ending with the fall of Corinth, and he chafed under the inglorious restraint, longing for the release of his energies, the larger life of the soldier, the opportunity for distinction. That opportunity, he felt, would come, as it comes to all in war time. Meanwhile he did what he could. No service was too humble for him to perform in aid of the South, no adventure too perilous for him to undertake if consistent with the character of a civilian who was at heart a soldier, and who in good faith and without too much qualification assented to at least a part of the frankly villainous dictum that all is fair in love and war.

One evening while Farquhar and his wife were sitting on a rustic bench near the entrance to his grounds, a gray-clad soldier rode up to the gate and asked for a drink of water. Mrs. Farquhar was only too happy to serve him with her own white hands. While she was fetching the water her husband approached the dusty horseman and inquired eagerly for news from the front.

"The Yanks are repairing the railroads," said the man, "and are getting ready for another advance. They have reached the Owl Creek bridge, put it in order and built a stockade on the north bank. The commandant has issued an order, which is posted everywhere, declaring that any civilian caught interfering with the railroad, its bridges, tunnels or trains will be summarily hanged. I saw the order."

"How far is it to the Owl Creek bridge?" Farquhar asked.

"About thirty miles."

"Is there no force on this side of the creek?"

"Only a picket post half a mile out, on the railroad, and a single sentinel at this end of the bridge."

"Suppose a man—a civilian and student of hanging —should elude the picket post and perhaps get the better of the sentinel," said Farquhar, smiling, "what could he accomplish?"

The soldier reflected. "I was there a month ago," he replied. "I observed that the flood of last winter had lodged a great quantity of driftwood against the wooden pier at this end of the bridge. It is now dry and would burn like tow."

The lady had now brought the water, which the soldier drank. He thanked her ceremoniously, bowed to her husband and rode away. An hour later, after nightfall, he repassed the plantation, going northward in the direction from which he had come. He was a Federal scout.

3

As Peyton Farquhar fell straight downward through the bridge he lost consciousness and was as one already dead. From this state he was awakened—ages later, it seemed to him—by the pain of a sharp pressure upon his throat, followed by a sense of suffocation. Keen, poignant agonies seemed to shoot from his neck downward through every fibre of his body and limbs. These pains appeared to flash along well-defined lines of ramification and to beat with an inconceivably rapid periodicity. They seemed like streams of pulsating fire heating him to an intolerable temperature. As to his head, he was conscious of nothing but a feeling of fulness—of congestion. These sensations were unaccompanied by thought. The intellectual part of his nature was already effaced; he had power only to feel, and feeling was torment. He was conscious of motion. Encompassed in a luminous cloud, of which he was now merely the fiery heart, without material substance, he swung through unthinkable arcs of oscillation, like a vast pendulum. Then all at once, with terrible suddenness, the light about him shot upward with the noise of a loud plash; a frightful roaring was in his ears, and all was cold and dark. The power of thought was restored; he knew that the rope had broken and he had fallen into the stream.

There was no additional strangulation; the noose about his neck was already suffocating him and kept the water from his lungs. To die of hanging at the bottom of a river!—the idea seemed to him ludicrous. He opened his eyes in the darkness and saw above him a gleam of light, but how distant, how inaccessible! He was still sinking, for the light became fainter and fainter until it was a mere glimmer. Then it began to grow and brighten, and he knew that he was rising toward the surface—knew it with reluctance, for he was now very comfortable. "To be hanged and drowned," he thought, "that is not so bad; but I do not wish to be shot. No; I will not be shot; that is not fair."

He was not conscious of an effort, but a sharp pain in his wrist apprised him that he was trying to free his hands. He gave the struggle his attention, as an idler might observe the feat of a juggler, without interest in the outcome. What splendid effort!—what magnificent, what superhuman strength! Ah, that was a fine endeavor! Bravo! The cord fell away; his arms parted and floated upward, the hands dimly seen on each side in the growing light. He watched them with a new interest as first one and then the other pounced upon the noose at his neck. They tore it away and thrust it fiercely aside, its undulations resembling those of a watersnake. "Put it back, put it back!" He thought he shouted these words to his hands, for the undoing of the noose had been succeeded by the direst pang that he had yet experienced. His neck ached horribly; his brain was on fire; his heart, which had been fluttering faintly, gave a great leap, trying to force itself out at his mouth. His whole body was racked and wrenched with an insupportable anguish! But his disobedient hands gave no heed to the command. They beat the water vigorously with quick, downward strokes, forcing him to the surface. He felt his head emerge; his eyes were blinded by the sunlight; his chest expanded convulsively, and with a supreme and crowning agony his lungs engulfed a great draught of air, which instantly he expelled in a shriek!

He was now in full possession of his physical senses. They were, indeed, preternaturally keen and alert. Something in the awful disturbance of his organic system had so exalted and refined them that they made record of things never before perceived. He felt the ripples upon his face and heard their separate sounds as they struck. He looked at the forest on the bank of the stream, saw the individual trees, the leaves and the veining of each leaf—saw the very insects upon them: the locusts, the brilliant-bodied flies, the gray spiders stretching their webs from twig to twig. He noted the prismatic colors in all the dewdrops upon a million blades of grass. The humming of the gnats that danced above the eddies of the stream, the beating of the dragon-flies' wings, the strokes of the water-spiders' legs, like oars which had lifted their boat—all these made audible music. A fish slid along beneath his eyes and he heard the rush of its body parting the water.

He had come to the surface facing down the stream; in a moment the visible world seemed to wheel slowly round, himself the pivotal point, and he saw the bridge, the fort, the soldiers upon the bridge, the captain, the sergeant, the two privates, his executioners. They were in silhouette against the blue sky. They shouted and gesticulated, pointing at him. The captain had drawn his pistol, but did not fire; the others were unarmed. Their movements were grotesque and horrible, their forms gigantic.

Suddenly he heard a sharp report and something struck the water smartly within a few inches of his head, spattering his face with spray. He heard a second report, and saw one of the sentinels with his rifle at his shoulder, a light cloud of blue smoke rising from the muzzle. The man in the water saw the eye of the man on the bridge gazing into his own through the sights of the rifle. He observed that it was a gray eye and remembered having read that gray eyes were keenest, and that all famous marksmen had them. Nevertheless, this one had missed.

A counter-swirl had caught Farquhar and turned him half round; he was again looking into the forest on the bank opposite the fort. The sound of a clear, high voice in a monotonous singsong now rang out behind him and came across the water with a distinctness that pierced and subdued all other sounds, even the beating of the ripples in his ears. Although no soldier, he had frequented camps enough to know the dread significance of that deliberate, drawling, aspirated chant; the lieutenant on shore was taking a part in the morning's work. How coldly and pitilessly—with what an even, calm intonation, presaging, and enforcing tranquility in the men—with what accurately measured intervals fell those cruel words:

"Attention, company! . . . Shoulder arms! . . . Ready! . . . Aim! . . . Fire!"

Farquhar dived—dived as deeply as he could. The water roared in his ears like the voice of Niagara, yet he heard the dulled thunder of the volley and, rising again toward the surface, met shining bits of metal, singularly flattened, oscillating slowly downward. Some of them touched him on the face and hands, then fell away, continuing their descent. One lodged between his collar and neck; it was uncomfortably warm and he snatched it out.

As he rose to the surface, gasping for breath, he

saw that he had been a long time under water; he was
perceptibly farther down stream—nearer to safety. The
soldiers had almost finished reloading; the metal
ramrods flashed all at once in the sunshine as they were
drawn from the barrels, turned in the air, and thrust
into their sockets. The two sentinels fired again, inde-
pendently and ineffectually.

The hunted man saw all this over his shoulder; he
was now swimming vigorously with the current. His
brain was as energetic as his arms and legs; he thought
with the rapidity of lightning.

"The officer," he reasoned, "will not make that
martinet's error a second time. It is as easy to dodge a
volley as a single shot. He has probably already given
the command to fire at will. God help me, I cannot
dodge them all!"

An appalling plash within two yards of him was
followed by a loud, rushing sound, *diminuendo*, which
seemed to travel back through the air to the fort and
died in an explosion which stirred the very river to its
deeps! A rising sheet of water curved over him, fell
down upon him, blinded him, strangled him! The cannon had taken a hand in the game. As he shook his
head free from the commotion of the smitten water he
heard the deflected shot humming through the air
ahead, and in an instant it was cracking and smashing
the branches in the forest beyond.

"They will not do that again," he thought; "the
next time they will use a charge of grape. I must keep
my eye upon the gun; the smoke will apprise me—the
report arrives too late; it lags behind the missile. That is
a good gun."

Suddenly he felt himself whirled round and round
—spinning like a top. The water, the banks, the forests,
the now distant bridge, fort and men—all were com-

mingled and blurred. Objects were represented by their colors only; circular horizontal streaks of color—that was all he saw. He had been caught in a vortex and was being whirled on with a velocity of advance and gyration that made him giddy and sick. In a few moments he was flung upon the gravel at the foot of the left bank of the stream—the southern bank—and behind a projecting point which concealed him from his enemies. The sudden arrest of his motion, the abrasion of one of his hands on the gravel, restored him, and he wept with delight. He dug his fingers into the sand, threw it over himself in handfuls and audibly blessed it. It looked like diamonds, rubies, emeralds; he could think of nothing beautiful which it did not resemble. The trees upon the bank were giant garden plants; he noted a definite order in their arrangement, inhaled the fragrance of their blooms. A strange, roseate light shone through the spaces among their trunks and the wind made in their branches the music of aeolian harps. He had no wish to perfect his escape—was content to remain in that enchanting spot until retaken.

A whiz and rattle of grapeshot among the branches high above his head roused him from his dream. The baffled cannoneer had fired him a random farewell. He sprang to his feet, rushed up the sloping bank, and plunged into the forest.

All that day he traveled, laying his course by the rounding sun. The forest seemed interminable; nowhere did he discover a break in it, not even a woodman's road. He had not known that he lived in so wild a region. There was something uncanny in the revelation.

By nightfall he was fatigued, footsore, famishing. The thought of his wife and children urged him on. At last he found a road which led him in what he knew to be the right direction. It was as wide and straight as a city street, yet it seemed untraveled. No fields bordered it, no dwelling anywhere. Not so much as the barking of a dog suggested human habitation. The black bodies of the trees formed a straight wall on both sides, terminating on the horizon in a point, like a diagram in a lesson in perspective. Overhead, as he looked up through this rift in the wood, shone great golden stars looking unfamiliar and grouped in strange constellations. He was sure they were arranged in some order which had a secret and malign significance. The wood on either side was full of singular noises, among which—once, twice, and again—he distinctly heard whispers in an unknown tongue.

His neck was in pain and lifting his hand to it he found it horribly swollen. He knew that it had a circle of black where the rope had bruised it. His eyes felt congested; he could no longer close them. His tongue was swollen with thirst; he relieved its fever by thrusting it forward from between his teeth into the cold air. How softly the turf had carpeted the untraveled avenue—he could no longer feel the roadway beneath his feet!

Doubtless, despite his suffering, he had fallen asleep while walking, for now he sees another scene— perhaps he has merely recovered from a delirium. He stands at the gate of his own home. All is as he left it, and all bright and beautiful in the morning sunshine. He must have traveled the entire night. As he pushes open the gate and passes up the wide white walk, he sees a flutter of female garments; his wife, looking fresh and cool and sweet, steps down from the veranda to meet him. At the bottom of the steps she stands waiting, with a smile of ineffable joy, an attitude of matchless grace and dignity. Ah, how beautiful she is! He springs forward with extended arms. As he is about to clasp her he feels a stunning blow upon the back of the neck; a blinding white light blazes all about him with a sound like the shock of a cannon—then all is darkness and silence!

Peyton Farquhar was dead; his body, with a broken neck, swung gently from side to side beneath the timbers of the Owl Creek bridge.

My Grandmother Millard and General Bedford Forrest and the Battle of Harrykin Creek

WILLIAM FAULKNER

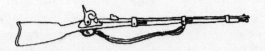

It would be right after supper, before we had left the table. At first, beginning with the day the news came that the Yankees had taken Memphis, we did it three nights in succession. But after that, as we got better and better and faster and faster, once a week suited Granny. Then after Cousin Melisandre finally got out of Memphis and came to live with us, it would be just once a month, and when the regiment in Virginia voted Father out of the colonelcy and he came home and stayed three months while he made a crop and got over his mad and organized his cavalry troop for General Forrest's command, we quit doing it at all. That is, we did it one time with Father there too, watching, and that night Ringo and I heard him laughing in the library, the first time he had laughed since he came home, until in about a half a minute Granny came out already holding her skirts up and went sailing up the stairs. So we didn't do it any more until Father had organized his troop and was gone again.

Granny would fold her napkin beside her plate. She would speak to Ringo standing behind her chair without even turning her head:

"Go call Joby and Lucius."

And Ringo would go back through the kitchen

without stopping. He would just say, "All right. Look out," at Louvinia's back and go to the cabin and come back with not only Joby and Lucius and the lighted lantern but Philadelphia too, even though Philadelphia wasn't going to do anything but stand and watch and then follow to the orchard and back to the house until Granny said we were done for that time and she and Lucius could go back home to bed. And we would bring down from the attic the big trunk (we had done it so many times by now that we didn't even need the lantern any more to go to the attic and get the trunk) whose lock it was my job to oil every Monday morning with a feather dipped in chicken fat, and Louvinia would come in from the kitchen with the unwashed silver from supper in a dishpan under one arm and the kitchen clock under the other and set the clock and the dishpan on the table and take from her apron pocket a pair of Granny's rolled-up stockings and hand them to Granny and Granny would unroll the stockings and take from the toe of one of them a wadded rag and open the rag and take out the key to the trunk and unpin her watch from her bosom and fold it into the rag and put the rag back into the stocking and roll the stockings back into a ball and put the ball into the trunk. Then with Cousin Melisandre and Philadelphia, watching, and Father too on that one time when he was there, Granny would stand facing the clock, her hands raised and about eight inches apart and her neck bowed she could watch the clock-face over her spectacles, until the big hand reached the nearest hour-mark.

The rest of us watched her hands. She wouldn't speak again. She didn't need to. There would be just the single light loud pop of her palms when the hand came to the nearest hour-mark; sometimes we would be already moving, even before her hands came together, all of us that is except Philadelphia. Granny wouldn't let her help at all, because of Lucius, even though Lucius had done nearly all the digging of the pit and did most of the carrying of the trunk each time. But Philadelphia had to be there. Granny didn't have to tell her but once. "I want the wives of all the free men here, too," Granny said. "I want all of you free folks to watch what the rest of us that ain't free have to do to keep that way."

That began about eight months ago. One day even I realized that something had happened to Lucius. Then I knew that Ringo had already seen it and that he knew what it was, so that when at last Louvinia came and told Granny, it was not as if Lucius had dared his mother to tell her but as if he had actually forced somebody, he didn't care who, to tell her. He had said it more than once, in the cabin one night probably for the first time, then after that in other places and to other people, to Negroes from other plantations even. Memphis was already gone then, and New Orleans, and all we had left of the River was Vicksburg and although we didn't believe it then, we wouldn't have that long. Then one morning Louvinia came in where Granny was cutting down the worn-out uniform pants Father had worn home from Virginia so they would fit me, and told Granny how Lucius was saying that soon the Yankees would have all of Mississippi and Yoknapatawpha County too and all the niggers would be free and that when that happened, he was going to be long gone. Lucius was working in the garden that morning. Granny went out to the back gallery, still carrying the pants and the needle. She didn't even push her spectacles up. She said, "You, Lucius," just once, and Lucius came out of the garden with the hoe and Granny stood looking down at him over the spectacles as she looked over them at everything she did, from reading or sewing to watching the clock-face until the instant came to start burying the silver.

"You can go now," she said. "You needn't wait on the Yankees."

"Go?" Lucius said. "I ain't free."

"You've been free for almost three minutes," Granny said. "Go on."

Lucius blinked his eyes while you could have counted about ten. "Go where?" he said.

"I can't tell you," Granny said. "I ain't free. I would imagine you will have all Yankeedom to move around in."

Lucius blinked his eyes. He didn't look at Granny now. "Was that all you wanted?" he said.

"Yes," Granny said. So he went back to the garden. And that was the last we heard about being free from him. That is, it quit showing in the way he acted, and if he talked any more of it, even Louvinia never thought it was worth bothering Granny with. It was Granny who would do the reminding of it, especially to Philadelphia, especially on the nights when we would stand like racehorses at the barrier, watching Granny's hands until they clapped together.

Each one of us knew exactly what he was to do. I would go upstairs for Granny's gold hatpin and her silver-headed umbrella and her plumed Sunday hat because she had already sent her ear-rings and brooch to Richmond a long time ago, and to Father's room for his silver-backed brushes and to Cousin Melisandre's room after she came to live with us for her things because the one time Granny let Cousin Melisandre try to help too, Cousin Melisandre brought all her dresses down. Ringo would go to the parlor for the candlesticks and Granny's dulcimer and the medallion of Father's mother back in Carolina. And we would run back to the dining-room where Louvinia and Lucius would have the side-board almost cleared, and Granny still standing there and watching the clock-face and the trunk both now with her hands ready to pop again and they would pop and Ringo and I would stop at the cellar door just long enough to snatch up the shovels and run on to the orchard and snatch the brush and grass and the criss-crossed sticks away and have the pit open and ready by the time we saw them coming: first Louvinia with the lantern, then Joby and Lucius with the trunk and Granny walking beside it and Cousin Melisandre and Philadelphia (and on that one time Father, walking along and laughing) following behind. And on that first night, the kitchen clock wasn't in the trunk. Granny was carrying it, while Louvinia held the lantern so that Granny could watch the hand, Granny made us put the trunk into the pit and grass back over it again and then dig up the trunk and carry it back to the house. And one night, it seemed like we had been bringing the trunk down from the attic and putting the silver into it and carrying it out to the pit and uncovering the pit and then covering the pit again and turning around and carrying the trunk back to the house and taking the silver out and putting it back where we got it from all winter and all summer, too;—that night, and I don't know who thought of it first, maybe it was all of us at once. But anyway the clock-hand had passed four hour-marks before Granny's hands even popped for Ringo and me to run and open the pit. And they came with the trunk and Ringo and I hadn't even put down the last armful of brush and sticks, to save having to stoop to pick it up again, and Lucius hadn't even put down his end of the trunk for the same reason and I reckon Louvinia was the only one that knew what was coming next because Ringo and I didn't know that the kitchen clock was still sitting on the dining-room table. Then Granny spoke. It was the first time we had ever heard her speak between when she would tell Ringo, "Go call Joby and Lucius," and then tell us both about thirty minutes later: "Wash your feet and go to bed." It was not loud and not long, just two words: "Bury it." And we lowered the trunk into the pit and Joby and Lucius threw the dirt back in and even then Ringo and I didn't move with the brush until Granny spoke again, not loud this time either: "Go on. Hide the pit." And we put the brush back and Granny said, "Dig it up." And we dug up the trunk and carried it back into the house and put the things back where we got them from and that was when I saw the kitchen clock still sitting on the dining-room table. And we all stood there watching Granny's hands until they popped together and that time we filled the trunk and carried it out to the orchard and lowered it into the pit quicker than we had ever done before.

2

And then when the time came to really bury the silver, it was too late. After it was all over and Cousin Melisandre and Cousin Philip were finally married and Father had got done laughing, Father said that always happened when a heterogeneous collection of people who were cohered simply by an uncomplex will for freedom engaged with a tyrannous machine. He said they would always lose the first battles, and if they were outnumbered and outweighed enough, it would seem to an outsider that they were going to lose them all. But they would not. They could not be defeated; if they just willed that freedom strongly and completely enough to sacrifice all else for it—ease and comfort and fatness of spirit and all, until whatever it was they had left would be enough, no matter how little it was—that very freedom itself would finally conquer the machine as a negative force like drouth or flood could strangle it. And later still, after two more years and we knew we were going to lose the war, he was still saying that. He said, "I won't see it but you will. You will see it in the next war, and in all the wars Americans will have to fight from then on. There will be men from the South in the forefront of all the battles, even leading some of them, helping those who conquered us defend that same freedom which they believed they had taken from us." And that happened: thirty years later, and General Wheeler, whom Father would have called apostate, commanding in Cuba, and whom old General Early did call apostate and matricide too in the office of the Richmond editor when he said: "I would like to have lived so that when my time comes, I will see Robert Lee again. But since I haven't, I'm certainly going to enjoy watching the devil burn that blue coat off Joe Wheeler."

We didn't have time. We didn't even know there were any Yankees in Jefferson, let alone within a mile of Sartoris. There never had been many. There was no railroad then and no river big enough for big boats and nothing in Jefferson they would have wanted even if they had come, since this was before Father had had time to worry them enough for General Grant to issue a general order with a reward for his capture. So we had got used to the war. We thought of it as being definitely fixed and established as a railroad or a river is, moving east along the railroad from Memphis and south along the River toward Vicksburg. We had heard tales of Yankee pillage and most of the people around Jefferson stayed ready to bury their silver fast too, though I don't reckon any of them practiced doing it like we did. But nobody we knew was even kin to anyone who had been pillaged, and so I don't think that even Lucius really expected any Yankees until that morning.

It was about eleven o'clock. The table was already set for dinner and everybody was beginning to kind of ease up so we would be sure to hear when Louvinia went out to the back gallery and rang the bell, when Ab Snopes came in at a dead run, on a strange horse as usual. He was a member of Father's troop. Not a fighting member; he called himself father's horse-captain, whatever he meant by it, though we had a pretty good idea, and none of us at least knew what he was doing in Jefferson when the troop was supposed to be up in Tennessee with General Bragg, and probably nobody anywhere knew the actual truth about how he got the horse, galloping across the yard and right through one of Granny's flower beds because I reckon he figures that carrying a message he could risk it, and on around to the back because he knew that, message or no message, he better not come to Granny's front door hollering that way, sitting that strange blown horse with a U. S. army brand on it you could read three hundred yards and yelling up at Granny that General Forrest was in Jefferson but there was a whole regiment of Yankee cavalry not a half a mile down the road.

So we never had time. Afterward Father admitted that Granny's error was not in strategy nor tactics either, even though she had copied from someone else. Because he said it had been a long time now since originality had been a component of military success. It just happened too fast. I went for Joby and Lucius and Philadelphia because Granny had already sent Ringo down to the road with a cup towel to wave when they came in sight. Then she sent me to the front window where I could watch Ringo. When Ab Snopes came back from hiding his new Yankee horse, he offered to go upstairs to get the things there. Granny had told us a long time ago never to let Ab Snopes go anywhere about the house unless somebody was with him. She said she would rather have Yankees in the house any day because at least Yankees would have more delicacy, even if it wasn't anything but good sense, than to steal a spoon or candlestick and then try to sell it to one of her own neighbors, as Ab Snopes would probably do. She didn't even answer him. She just said, "Stand over there by that door and be quiet." So Cousin Melisandre went upstairs after all and Granny and Philadelphia went to the parlor for the candlesticks and the medallion and the dulcimer, Philadelphia not only helping this time, free or not, but Granny wasn't even using the clock.

It just all happened at once. One second Ringo was sitting on the gate-post, looking up the road. The next second he was standing on it and waving the cup towel and then I was running and hollering, back to the dining-room, and I remember the whites of Joby's and Lucius's and Philadelphia's eyes and I remember Cousin Melisandre's eyes where she leaned against the sideboard with the back of her hand against her mouth, and Granny and Louvinia and Ab Snopes glaring at one another across the trunk and I could hear Louvinia's voice even louder than mine:

"Miz Cawmpson! Miz Cawmpson!"

"What?" Granny cried. "What? Mrs. Compson?" Then we all remembered. It was when the first Yankee scouting patrol entered Jefferson over a year ago. The war was new then and I suppose General Compson was the only Jefferson soldier they had heard of yet. Anyway, the officer asked someone in the Square where General Compson lived and old Doctor Holston sent his Negro boy by back alleys and across lots to warn Mrs. Compson in time, and the story was how the Yankee officer sent some of his men through the empty house and himself rode around to the back where old Aunt Roxanne was standing in front of the outhouse behind the closed door of which Mrs. Compson was sitting, fully dressed even to her hat and parasol, on the wicker hamper containing her plate and silver. "Miss in dar," Roxanne said. "Stop where you is." And the story told how the Yankee officer said, "Excuse me," and raised his hat and even backed the horse a few steps before he turned and called his men and rode away. "The privy!" Granny cried.

"Hell fire, Miz Millard!" Ab Snopes said. And Granny never said anything. It wasn't like she didn't hear, because she was looking right at him. It was like she didn't care; that she might have even said it herself. And that shows how things were then: we just never had time for anything. "Hell fire," Ab Snopes said, "all north Missippi has done heard about that! There ain't a white lady between here and Memphis that ain't setting in the back house on a grip full of silver right this minute."

"Then we're already late," Granny said. "Hurry."

"Wait!" Ab Snopes said. "Wait! Even the Yankees have done caught on to that by now!"

"Then let's hope these are different Yankees," Granny said. "Hurry."

"But Miz Millard!" Ab Snopes cried. "Wait! Wait!"

But then we could hear Ringo yelling down at the gate and I remember Joby and Lucius and Philadelphia and Louvinia and the balloon-like swaying of Cousin Melisandre's skirts as they ran across the back yard, the trunk somewhere among them; I remember how Joby and Lucius tumbled the trunk into the little tall narrow flimsy sentry-box and Louvinia thrust Cousin Melisandre in and slammed the door and we could hear Ringo

yelling good now, almost to the house, and then I was
back at the front window and I saw them just as they
swept around the house in a kind of straggling-clump—
six men in blue, riding fast yet with something curious
in the action of the horses, as if they were not only
yoked together in spans but were hitched to a single
wagon-tongue, then Ringo on foot running and not yelling now, and last of all the seventh rider, bareheaded
and standing in his stirrups and with a sabre over his
head. Then I was on the back gallery again, standing
beside Granny above that moil of horses and men in the
yard, and she was wrong. It was as if these were not
only the same ones who had been at Mrs. Compson's
last year, but somebody had even told them exactly
where our outhouse was. The horses were yoked in
pairs, but it was not a wagon-tongue, it was a pole, almost a log, twenty feet long, slung from saddle to saddle between the three span; and I remember the faces,
unshaven and wan and not so much peering as frantically gleeful, glaring up at us for an instant before the
men leaped down and unslung the pole and jerked the
horses aside and picked up the pole, three to a side, and
began to run across the yard with it as the last rider
came around the house, in gray (an officer: it was
Cousin Philip, though of course we didn't know that
then, and there was going to be a considerable more
uproar and confusion before he finally became Cousin
Philip and of course we didn't know that either), the
sabre still lifted and not only standing in the stirrups
but almost lying down along the horse's neck. The six
Yankees never saw him. And we used to watch Father
drilling his troop in the pasture, changing them from
column to troop front at full gallop, and you could hear
his voice even above the sound of the galloping hooves
but it wasn't a bit louder than Granny's. "There's a lady

in there!" she said. But the Yankees never heard her any more than they had seen Cousin Philip yet, the whole mass of them, the six men running with the pole and Cousin Philip on the horse, leaning out above them with a lifted sabre, rushing on across the yard until the end of the pole struck the outhouse door. It didn't just overturn, it exploded. One second it stood there, tall and narrow and flimsy; the next second it was gone and there was a boil of yelling men in blue coats darting and dodging around under Cousin Philip's horse and the flashing sabre until they could find a chance to turn and run. Then there was a scatter of planks and shingles and Cousin Melisandre sitting beside the trunk in the middle of it, in the spread of her hoops, her eyes shut and her mouth open, still screaming, and after a while a feeble popping of pistol-shots from down along the creek that didn't sound any more like war than a boy with firecrackers.

"I tried to tell you to wait!" Ab Snopes said behind us, "I tried to tell you them Yankees had done caught on!"

After Joby and Lucius and Ringo and I finished burying the trunk in the pit and hiding the shovel-marks, I found Cousin Philip in the summer house. His sabre and belt were propped against the wall but I don't reckon even he knew what had become of his hat. He had his coat off too and was wiping it with his handkerchief and watching the house with one eye around the edge of the door. When I came in he straightened up and I thought at first he was looking at me. Then I don't know what he was looking at. "That beautiful girl," he said. "Fetch me a comb."

"They're waiting for you in the house," I said. "Granny wants to know what's the matter." Cousin Melisandre was all right now. It took Louvinia and Philadelphia both and finally Granny to get her into the house but Louvinia brought the elder-flower wine before Granny had time to send her after it and now Cousin Melisandre and Granny were waiting in the parlor.

"Your sister," Cousin Philip said. "And a hand-mirror."

"No, Sir," I said. "She's just our cousin. From Memphis. Granny says—" Because he didn't know Granny. It was pretty good for her to wait any time for anybody. But he didn't even let me finish.

"That beautiful, tender girl," he said. "And send a nigger with a basin of water and a towel." I went back toward the house. This time when I looked back I couldn't see his eye around the door-edge. "And a clothes brush," he said.

Granny wasn't waiting very much. She was at the front door. "Now what?" she said. I told her. "Does the man think we are giving a ball here in the middle of the day? Tell him I said to come on in and wash on the back gallery like we do. Louvinia's putting dinner on, and we're already late." But Granny didn't know Cousin Philip either. I told her again. She looked at me. "What did he say?" she said.

"He didn't say anything," I said. "Just that beautiful girl."

"That's all he said to me too," Ringo said. I hadn't heard him come in. "Sides the soap and water. Just that beautiful girl."

"Was he looking at you either when he said it?" I said.

"No," Ringo said. "I just thought for a minute he was."

Now Granny looked at Ringo and me both. "Hah," she said, and afterward when I was older I found out that Granny already knew Cousin Philip too, that she could look at one of them and know all the other Cousin Melisandres and Cousin Philips both without having to see them. "I sometimes think that bullets are just about the least fatal things that fly, especially in war.—All right," she said. "Take him his soap and water. But hurry."

We did. This time he didn't say "that beautiful girl." He said it twice. He took off his coat and handed it to Ringo. "Brush it good," he said. "Your sister, I heard you say."

"No, you didn't," I said.

"No matter," he said. "I want a nosegay. To carry in my hand."

"Those flowers are Granny's," I said.

"No matter," he said. He rolled up his sleeves and began to wash. "A small one. About a dozen blooms. Get something pink."

I went and got the flowers. I don't know whether Granny was still at the front door or not. Maybe she wasn't. At least she never said anything. So I picked the ones Ab Snopes' new Yankee horse had already trampled down and wiped the dirt off of them and straightened them out and went back to the summer house where Ringo was holding the hand-glass while Cousin Philip combed his hair. Then he put on his coat and buckled on his sabre again and held his feet out one at a time for Ringo to wipe his boots off with the towel, and Ringo saw it. I wouldn't have spoken at all because we were already later for dinner than ever now, even if there hadn't never been a Yankee on the place. "You tore your britches on them Yankees," Ringo said.

So I went back to the house. Granny was standing in the hall. This time she just said, "Yes?" It was almost quiet.

"He tore his britches," I said. And she knew more about Cousin Philip than even Ringo could find out by looking at him. She had the needle already threaded in the bosom of her dress. And I went back to the summer house and then we came back to the house and up to the front door and I waited for him to go into the hall but he didn't, he just stood there holding the nosegay in one hand and his hat in the other, not very old, looking at that moment anyway not very much older than Ringo and me for all his braid and sash and sabre and boots and spurs, and even after just two years looking like all our soldiers and most of the other people too did: as if it had been so long now since he had had all he wanted to eat at one time that even his memory and palate had forgotten it and only his body remembered, standing there with his nosegay and that beautiful-girl look in his face like he couldn't have seen anything even if he had been looking at it.

"No," he said. "Announce me. It should be your nigger. But no matter." He said his full name, all three of them, twice, as if he thought I might forget them before I could reach the parlor.

"Go on in," I said. "They're waiting for you. They had already been waiting for you even before you found your pants were torn."

"Announce me," he said. He said his name again. "Of Tennessee. Lieutenant, Savage's Battalion, Forrest's Command, Provisional Army, Department of the West."

So I did. We crossed the hall to the parlor, where Granny stood between Cousin Melisandre's chair and the table where the decanter of elder-flower wine and three fresh glasses and even a plate of the tea cakes Louvinia had learned to make from cornmeal and molasses were sitting, and he stopped again at that door too and I know he couldn't even see Cousin Melisandre

for a minute, even though he never had looked at anything else but her. "Lieutenant Philip St-Just Backhouse," I said. I said it loud, because he had repeated it
to me three times so I would be sure to get it right and I
wanted to say it to suit him too since even if he had
made us a good hour late for dinner, at least he had
saved the silver. "Of Tennessee," I said. "Savage's Battalion, Forrest's Command, Provisional Army, Department of the West."

While you could count maybe five, there wasn't
anything at all. Then Cousin Melisandre screamed. She
sat bolt upright on the chair like she had sat beside the
trunk in the litter of planks and shingles in the back
yard this morning, with her eyes shut and her mouth
open again, screaming.

3

So we were still another half an hour late for dinner.
Though this time it never needed anybody but Cousin
Philip to get Cousin Melisandre upstairs. All he needed
to do was try to speak to her again. Then Granny came
back down and said, "Well, if we don't want to just quit
and start calling it supper, we'd better walk in and eat it
within the next hour and a half at least." So we walked
in. Ab Snopes was already waiting in the dining-room. I
reckon he had been waiting longer than anybody, because after all Cousin Melisandre wasn't any kin to him.
Ringo drew Granny's chair and we sat down. Some of it
was cold. The rest of it had been on the stove so long
now that when you ate it it didn't matter whether it was
cold or not. But Cousin Philip didn't seem to mind. And
maybe it didn't take his memory very long to remember
again what it was like to have all he wanted to eat, but I
don't think his palate ever tasted any of it. He would sit

there eating like he hadn't seen any food of any kind in at least a week, and like he was expecting what was even already on his fork to vanish before he could get it into his mouth. Then he would stop with the fork halfway to his mouth and sit there looking at Cousin Melisandre's empty place, laughing. That is, I don't know what else to call it but laughing. Until at last I said,

"Why don't you change your name?"

Then Granny quit eating too. She looked at me over her spectacles. Then she took both hands and lifted the spectacles up her nose until she could look at me through them. Then she even pushed the spectacles up into her front hair and looked at me. "That's the first sensible thing I've heard said on this place since eleven o'clock this morning," she said. "It's so sensible and simple that I reckon only a child could have thought of it." She looked at him. "Why don't you?"

He laughed some more. That is, his face did the same way and he made the same sound again. "My grandfather was at King's Mountain, with Marion all through Carolina. My uncle was defeated for Governor of Tennessee by a corrupt and traitorous cabal of tavernkeepers and Republican Abolitionists, and my father died at Chapultepec. After that, the name they bore is not mine to change. Even my life is not mine so long as my country lies bleeding and ravished beneath an invader's iron heel." Then he stopped laughing, or whatever it was. Then his face looked surprised. Then it quit looking surprised, the surprise fading out of it steady at first and gradually faster but not very much faster like the heat fades out of a piece of iron on a blacksmith's anvil until his face just looked amazed and quiet and almost peaceful. "Unless I lose it in battle," he said.

"You can't very well do that sitting here," Granny said.

"No," he said. But I don't think he even heard her except with his ears. He stood up. Even Ab Snopes was watching him now, his knife stopped halfway to his mouth with a wad of greens on the end of the blade. "Yes," Cousin Philip said. His face even had the beautiful-girl look on it again. "Yes," he said. He thanked Granny for his dinner. That is, I reckon that's what he had told his mouth to say. It didn't make much sense to us, but I don't think he was paying any attention to it at all. He bowed. He wasn't looking at Granny nor at anything else. He said "Yes" again. Then he went out. Ringo and I followed to the front door and watched him mount his horse and sit there for a minute, bareheaded, looking up at the upstairs windows. It was Granny's room he was looking at, with mine and Ringo's room next to it. But Cousin Melisandre couldn't have seen him even if she had been in either one of them, since she was in bed on the other side of the house with Philadelphia probably still wringing the cloths out in cold water to lay on her head. He sat the horse well. He rode it well, too: light and easy and back in the saddle and toes in perpendicular from ankle to knee as Father had taught me. It was a good horse too.

"It's a damn good horse," I said.

"Git the soap," Ringo said.

But even then I looked quick back down the hall, even if I could hear Granny talking to Ab Snopes in the dining-room. "She's still in there," I said.

"Hah," Ringo said. "I done tasted soap in my mouth for a cuss I thought was a heap further off than that."

Then Cousin Philip spurred the horse and was gone. Or so Ringo and I thought. Two hours ago none of us had ever even heard of him; Cousin Melisandre had seen him twice and sat with her eyes shut screaming both times. But after we were older, Ringo and I realized that Cousin Philip was probably the only one in the whole lot of us that really believed even for one moment that he had said goodbye forever, that not only Granny and Louvinia knew better but Cousin Melisandre did too, no matter what his last name had the bad luck to be.

We went back to the dining-room. Then I realized that Ab Snopes had been waiting for us to come back. Then we both knew he was going to ask Granny something because nobody wanted to be alone when they had to ask Granny something even when they didn't know they were going to have trouble with it. We had known Ab for over a year now. I should have known what it was like Granny already did. He stood up. "Well, Miz Millard," he said. "I figger you'll be safe all right from now on, with Bed Forrest and his boys right there in Jefferson. But until things quiet down a mite more, I'll just leave the horses in your lot for a day or two."

"What horses?" Granny said. She and Ab didn't just look at one another. They watched one another.

"Them fresh-captured horses from this morning," Ab said.

"What horses?" Granny said. Then Ab said it.

"My horses." Ab watched her.

"Why?" Granny said. But Ab knew what she meant.

"I'm the only grown man here," he said. Then he said, "I seen them first. They were chasing me before—" Then he said, talking fast now; his eyes had gone kind of glazed for a second but now they were bright again, looking in the stubbly dirty-colored fuzz on his face like two chips of broken plate in a worn-out door-mat: "Spoils of war! I brought them here! I tolled them in here: a military and-bush! And as the only and ranking Confedrit military soldier present—"

"You ain't a soldier," Granny said. "You stipulated that to Colonel Sartoris yourself while I was listening. You told him yourself you would be his independent horse-captain but nothing more."

"Ain't that just exactly what I am trying to be?" he said. "Didn't I bring all six of them horses in here in my own possession, the same as if I was leading them on a rope?"

"Hah," Granny said. "A spoil of war or any other kind of spoil don't belong to a man or a woman either until they can take it home and put it down and turn their back on it. You never had time to get home with even the one you were riding. You ran in the first open gate you came to, no matter whose gate it was."

"Except it was the wrong one," he said. His eyes quit looking like china. They didn't look like anything. But I reckon his face would still look like an old door-mat even after he had turned all the way white. "So I reckon I got to even walk back to town," he said. "The woman that would . . ." His voice stopped. He and Granny looked at one another.

"Don't you say it," Granny said.

"Nome," he said. He didn't say it. ". . . a man of seven horses ain't likely to lend him a mule."

We all went out to the lot. I don't reckon that even Ab knew until then that Granny had already found where he thought he had hidden the first horse and had it brought up to the lot with the other six. But at least he already had his saddle and bridle with him. But it was too late. Six of the horses moved about loose in the lot. The seventh one was tied just inside the gate with a piece of plow-line. It wasn't the horse Ab had come on because that horse had a blaze. Ab had known Granny long enough too. He should have known. Maybe he did. But at least he tried. He opened the gate.

"Well," he said, "it ain't getting no earlier. I reckon I better—"

"Wait," Granny said. Then we looked at the horse which was tied to the fence. At first glance it looked the best one of the seven. You had to see it just right to tell its near leg was sprung a little, maybe from being worked too hard too young under too much weight. "Take that one," Granny said.

"That ain't mine," Ab said. "That's one of yourn. I'll just—"

"Take that one," Granny said. Ab looked at her. You could have counted at least ten.

"Hell fire, Miz Millard," he said.

"I've told you before about cursing on this place," Granny said.

"Yessum," Ab said. Then he said it again: "Hell fire." He went into the lot and rammed the bit into the tied horse's mouth and clapped the saddle on and snatched the piece of plow-line off and threw it over the fence and got up and Granny stood there until he had ridden out of the lot and Ringo closed the gate and that was the first time I noticed the chain and padlock from the smokehouse door and Ringo locked it and handed Granny the key and Ab sat for a minute, looking down at her. "Well, good-day," he said. "I just hope for the sake of the Confedricy that Bed Forrest don't never tangle with you with all the horses he's got." Then he said it again, maybe worse this time because now he was already on a horse pointed toward the gate: "Or you'll damn shore leave him just one more passel of infantry before he can spit twice."

Then he was gone too. Except for hearing Cousin Melisandre now and then, and those six horses with

U.S. branded on their hips standing in the lot, it might never have happened. At least Ringo and I thought that was all of it. Every now and then Philadelphia would come downstairs with the pitcher and draw some more cold water for Cousin Melisandre's cloths but we thought that after a while even that would just wear out and quit. Then Philadelphia came down again and came in to where Granny was cutting down a pair of Yankee pants that Father had worn home last time so they would fit Ringo. She didn't say anything. She just stood in the door until Granny said, "All right. What now?"

"She want the banjo," Philadelphia said.

"What?" Granny said. "My dulcimer? She can't play it. Go back upstairs."

But Philadelphia didn't move. "Could I ax Mammy to come help me?"

"No," Granny said. "Louvinia's resting. She's had about as much of this as I want her to stand. Go back upstairs. Give her some more wine if you can't think of anything else." And she told Ringo and me to go somewhere else, anywhere else, but even in the yard you could still hear Cousin Melisandre talking to Philadelphia. And once we even heard Granny though it was still mostly Cousin Melisandre telling Granny that she had already forgiven her, that nothing whatever had happened and that all she wanted now was peace. And after a while Louvinia came up from the cabin without even being sent for and went upstairs and then it began to look like we were going to be late for supper too. But Philadelphia finally came down and cooked it and carried Cousin Melisandre's tray up and then we quit eating; we could hear Louvinia overhead, in Granny's room now, and she came down and set the untasted tray on the table and stood beside Granny's chair with the key to the trunk in her hand.

"All right," Granny said. "Go call Joby and Lucius." We got the lantern and the shovels. We went to the orchard and removed the brush and dug up the trunk and got the dulcimer and buried the trunk and put the brush back and brought the key in to Granny. And Ringo and I could hear her from our room and Granny was right. We heard her for a long time and Granny was surely right; she just never said but half of it. The moon came up after a while and we could look down from our window into the garden, at Cousin Melisandre sitting on the bench with the moonlight glinting on the pearl inlay of the dulcimer, and Philadelphia squatting on the sill of the gate with her apron over her head. Maybe she was asleep. It was already late. But I don't see how.

So we didn't hear Granny until she was already in the room, her shawl over her nightgown and carrying a candle. "In a minute I'm going to have about all of this I aim to stand too," she said. "Go wake Lucius and tell him to saddle the mule," she told Ringo. "Bring me the pen and ink and a sheet of paper." I fetched them. She didn't sit down. She stood up at the bureau while I held the candle, writing even and steady and not very much, and signed her name and let the paper lie open to dry until Lucius came in. "Ab Snopes said that Mr. Forrest is in Jefferson," she told Lucius. "Find him. Tell him I will expect him here for breakfast in the morning and to bring that boy." She used to know General Forrest in Memphis before he got to be a general. He used to trade with Grandfather Millard's supply house and sometimes he would come out to sit with Grandfather on the front gallery and sometimes he would eat with them. "You can tell him I have six captured horses for him," she said. "And never mind patter-rollers or soldiers either. Haven't you got my signature on that paper?"

"I ain't worrying about them," Lucius said. "But suppose them Yankees—"

"I see," Granny said. "Hah. I forgot. You've been waiting for Yankees, haven't you? But those this morning seemed to be too busy trying to stay free to have much time to talk about it, didn't they?—Get along," she said. "Do you think any Yankee is going to dare ignore what a Southern soldier or even a patter-roller wouldn't—And you go to bed," she said.

We lay down, both of us on Ringo's pallet. We heard the mule when Lucius left. Then we heard the mule and at first we didn't know we had been asleep, the mule coming back now and the moon had started down the west and Cousin Melisandre and Philadelphia were gone from the garden, to where Philadelphia at least could sleep better than sitting on a square sill with an apron over her head, or at least where it was quieter. And we heard Lucius fumbling up the stairs but we never heard Granny at all because she was already at the top of the stairs, talking down at the noise Lucius was trying not to make. "Speak up," she said. "I ain't asleep but I ain't a lip-reader either. Not in the dark."

"Genl Fawhrest say he respectful compliments," Lucius said, "and he can't come to breakfast this morning because he gonter to be whuppin Genl Smith at Tallahatchie Crossing about that time. But providin' he ain't too fur away in the wrong direction when him and Genl Smith git done, he be proud to accept your invitation next time he in the neighborhood. And he say 'whut boy.' "

While you could count about five, Granny didn't say anything. Then she said, "What?"

"He say 'whut boy,' " Lucius said.

Then you could have counted ten. All we could

hear was Lucius breathing. Then Granny said: "Did you wipe the mule down?"

"Yessum," Lucius said.

"Did you turn her back into the pasture?"

"Yessum," Lucius said.

"Then go to bed," Granny said. "And you too," she said.

General Forrest found out what boy. This time we didn't know we had been asleep either, and it was no one mule now. The sun was just rising. When we heard Granny and scrambled to the window, yesterday wasn't a patch on it. There were at least fifty of them now, in gray; the whole outdoors was full of men on horses, with Cousin Philip out in front of them, sitting his horse in almost exactly the same spot where he had been yesterday, looking up at Granny's window and not seeing it or anything else this time either. He had a hat now. He was holding it clamped over his heart and he hadn't shaved and yesterday he had looked younger than Ringo because Ringo always had looked about ten years older than me. But now, with the first sun-ray making a little soft fuzz in the gold-colored stubble on his face, he looked even younger than I did, and gaunt and worn in the face like he hadn't slept any last night and something else in his face too: like he not only hadn't slept any last night but by godfrey he wasn't going to sleep tonight either as long as he had anything to do with it. "Goodbye," he said. "Goodbye," and whirled his horse, spurring, and raised the new hat over his head like he had carried the sabre yesterday and the whole mass of them went piling back across flower beds and lawn and all and back down the drive toward the gate while Granny still stood at her window in her nightgown, her voice louder than any man's anywhere, I don't care who

he is or what he would be doing: "Backhouse! Backhouse! You, Backhouse!"

So we ate breakfast early. Granny sent Ringo in his
nightshirt to wake Louvinia and Lucius both. So Lucius
had the mule saddled before Louvinia even got the fire
lit. This time Granny didn't write a note. "Go to Tallahatchie Crossing," she told Lucius. "Sit there and wait
for him if necessary."

"Suppose they done already started the battle?"
Lucius said.

"Suppose they have?" Granny said. "What busi-
ness is that of yours or mine either? You find Bedford
Forrest. Tell him this is important; it won't take long.
But don't you show your face here again without him."

Lucius rode away. He was gone four days. He
didn't even get back in time for the wedding, coming
back up the drive about sundown on the fourth day
with two soldiers in one of General Forrest's forage
wagons with the mule tied to the tailgate. He didn't
know where he had been and he never did catch up
with the battle. "I never even heard it," he told Joby
and Louvinia and Philadelphia and Ringo and me. "If
wars always moves that far and that fast, I don't see
how they ever have time to fight."

But it was all over then. It was the second day, the
day after Lucius left. It was just after dinner this time
and by now we were used to soldiers. But these were
different, just five of them, and we never had seen just
that few of them before and we had come to think of
soldiers as either jumping on and off horses in the yard
or going back and forth through Granny's flower beds
at full gallop. These were all officers and I reckon
maybe I hadn't seen so many soldiers after all because I
never saw this much braid before. They came up the
drive at a trot, like people just taking a ride, and

stopped without trompling even one flower bed and General Forrest got down and came up the walk toward where Granny waited on the front gallery—a big, dusty man with a big beard so black it looked almost blue and eyes like a sleepy owl, already taking off his hat. "Well, Miss Rosie," he said.

"Don't call me Rosie," Granny said. "Come in. Ask your gentlemen to alight and come in."

"They'll wait there," General Forrest said. "We are a little rushed. My plans have . . ." Then we were in the library. He wouldn't sit down. He looked tired all right, but there was something else a good deal livelier than just tired. "Well, Miss Rosie," he said. "I—"

"Don't call me Rosie," Granny said. "Can't you ever say Rosa?"

"Yessum," he said. But he couldn't. At least, he never did. "I reckon we both have had about enough of this. That boy—"

"Hah," Granny said. "Night before last you were saying what boy. Where is he? I sent you word to bring him with you."

"Under arrest," General Forrest said. It was a considerable more than just tired. "I spent four days getting Smith just where I wanted him. After that, this boy here could have fought the battle." He said 'fit' for fought just as he said 'druv' for drove and 'drug' for dragged. But maybe when you fought battles like he did, even Granny didn't mind how you talked. "I won't bother you with details. He didn't know them either. All he had to do was exactly what I told him. I did everything but draw a diagram on his coat-tail of exactly what he was to do, no more and no less, from the time he left me until he saw me again: which was to make contact and then fall back. I gave him just exactly the right number of men so that he couldn't do anything else but that. I told him exactly how fast to fall back and how much racket to make doing it and even how to make the racket. But what do you think he did?"

"I can tell you," Granny said. "He sat on his horse at five o'clock yesterday morning, with my whole yard full of men behind him, yelling goodbye at my window."

"He divided his men and sent half of them into the bushes to make a noise and took the other half who were the nearest to complete fools and led a sabre charge on that outpost. He didn't fire a shot. He drove it clean back with sabres into Smith's main body and scared Smith so that he threw out all his cavalry and pulled out behind it and now I don't know whether I'm about to catch him or he's about to catch me. My provost finally caught the boy last night. He had come back and got the other thirty men of his company and was twenty miles ahead again, trying to find something to lead another charge against. 'Do you want to be killed?' I said. 'Not especially,' he said. 'That is, I don't especially care one way or the other.' 'Then neither do I,' I said. 'But you risked a whole company of my men.' 'Ain't that what they enlisted for?' he said. 'They enlisted into a military establishment the purpose of which is to expend each man only at a profit. Or maybe you don't consider me a shrewd enough trader in human meat?' 'I can't say,' he said. 'Since day before yesterday I ain't thought very much about how you or anybody else runs this war.' 'And just what were you doing day before yesterday that changed your ideas and habits?' I said. 'Fighting some of it,' he said. 'Dispersing the enemy.' 'Where?' I said. 'At a lady's house a few miles from Jefferson,' he said. 'One of the niggers called her Granny like the white boy did. The others called her

Miss Rosie.' " This time Granny didn't say anything. She just waited.

"Go on," she said.

" 'I'm still trying to win battles, even if since day before yesterday you ain't,' I said. 'I'll send you down to Johnston at Jackson,' I said. 'He'll put you inside Vicksburg, where you can lead private charges day and night too if you want.' 'Like hell you will,' he said. And I said—excuse me—'Like hell I won't.' " And Granny didn't say anything. It was like day before yesterday with Ab Snopes: not like she hadn't heard but as if right now it didn't matter, that this was no time either to bother with such.

"And did you?" she said.

"I can't. He knows it. You can't punish a man for routing an enemy four times his weight. What would I say back in Tennessee, where we both live, let alone that uncle of his, the one they licked for Governor six years ago, on Bragg's personal staff now with his face over Bragg's shoulder every time Bragg opens a dispatch or picks up a pen. And I'm still trying to win battles. But I can't. Because of a girl, one single lone young female girl that ain't got anything under the sun against him except that, since it was his misfortune to save her from a passel of raiding enemy in a situation that everybody but her is trying to forget, she can't seem to bear his last name. Yet because of that, every battle I plan from now on will be at the mercy of a twenty-two-year-old shave-tail—excuse me again—who might decide to lead a private charge any time he can holler at least two men in gray coats into moving in the same direction." He stopped. He looked at Granny. "Well?" he said.

"So now you've got to it," Granny said. "Well what, Mr. Forrest?"

"Why, just have done with this foolishness. I told

you I've got that boy, in close arrest, with a guard with a bayonet. But there won't be any trouble there. I figured even yesterday morning that he had already lost his mind. But I reckon he's recovered enough of it since the Provost took him last night to comprehend that I still consider myself his commander even if he don't. So all that's necessary now is for you to put your foot down. Put it down hard. Now. You're her grandma. She lives in your home. And it looks like she is going to live in it a good while yet before she gets back to Memphis to that uncle or whoever it is that calls himself her guardian. So just put your foot down. Make her. Mr. Millard would have already done that if he had been here. And I know when. It would have been two days ago by now."

Granny waited until he got done. She stood with her arms crossed, holding each elbow in the other. "Is that all I'm to do?" she said.

"Yes," General Forrest said. "If she don't want to listen to you right at first, maybe as his commander—"

Granny didn't even say "Hah." She didn't even send me. She didn't even stop in the hall and call. She went upstairs herself and we stood there and I thought maybe she was going to bring the dulcimer too and I thought how if I was General Forrest I would go back and get Cousin Philip and make him sit in the library until about supper-time while Cousin Melisandre played the dulcimer and sang. Then he could take Cousin Philip on back and then he could finish the war without worrying.

She didn't have the dulcimer. She just had Cousin Melisandre. They came in and Granny stood to one side again with her arms crossed, holding her elbows. "Here she is," she said. "Say it—This is Mr. Bedford Forrest," she told Cousin Melisandre. "Say it," she told General Forrest.

He didn't have time. When Cousin Melisandre first came, she tried to read aloud to Ringo and me. It wasn't much. That is, what she insisted on reading to us wasn't so bad, even if it was mostly about ladies looking out windows and playing on something (maybe they were dulcimers too) while somebody else was off somewhere fighting. It was the way she read it. When Granny said this is Mister Forrest, Cousin Melisandre's face looked exactly like her voice would sound when she read to us. She took two steps into the library and curtsied, spreading her hoops back, and stood up. "General Forrest," she said. "I am acquainted with an associate of his. Will the General please give him the sincerest wishes for triumph in war and success in love, from one who will never see him again?" Then she curtsied again and spread her hoops backward and stood up and took two steps backward and turned and went out.

After a while Granny said, "Well, Mr. Forrest?"

General Forrest began to cough. He lifted his coattail with one hand and reached the other into his hip pocket like he was going to pull at least a musket out of it and got his handkerchief and coughed into it a while. It wasn't very clean. It looked about like the one Cousin Philip was trying to wipe his coat off with in the summer house day before yesterday. Then he put the handkerchief back. He didn't say "Hah" either. "Can I reach the Holly Branch road without having to go through Jefferson?" he said.

Then Granny moved. "Open the desk," she said. "Lay out a sheet of note-paper." I did. And I remember how I stood at one side of the desk and General Forrest at the other, and watched Granny's hand move the pen steady and not very slow and not very long across the paper because it never did take her very long to say anything, no matter what it was, whether she was talking it or writing it. Though I didn't see it then, but only later, when it hung framed under glass above Cousin Melisandre's and Cousin Philip's mantel: the fine steady slant of Granny's hand and General Forrest's sprawling signatures below it that looked itself a good deal like a charge of massed calvary:

Lieutenant P. S. Backhouse, Company D, Tennessee Cavalry, was this day raised to the honorary rank of Brevet Major General and killed while engaging the enemy. Vice whom Philip St-Just Backus is hereby appointed Lieutenant, Company D, Tennessee Cavalry.

N. B. Forrest Genl

I didn't see it then. General Forrest picked it up. "Now I've got to have a battle," he said. "Another sheet, son." I laid that one out on the desk.

"A battle?" Granny said.

"To give Johnston," he said. "Confound it, Miss Rosie, can't you understand either than I'm just a fallible mortal man trying to run a military command according to certain fixed and inviolable rules, no matter how foolish the business looks to superior outside folks?"

"All right," Granny said. "You had one. I was looking at it."

"So I did," General Forrest said. "Hah," he said. "The battle of Sartoris."

"No," Granny said. "Not at my house."

"They did all the shooting down at the creek," I said.

"What creek?" he said.

So I told him. It ran through the pasture. Its name

was Hurricane Creek but not even the white people called it hurricane except Granny. General Forrest didn't either when he sat down at the desk and wrote the report to General Johnston at Jackson:

A unit of my command on detached duty engaged a body of the enemy and drove him from the field and dispersed him this day 28th ult. April 1863 at Harrykin Creek. With loss of one man.

N. B. Forrest Genl

I saw that. I watched him write it. Then he got up and folded the sheets into his pocket and was already going toward the table where his hat was.

"Wait," Granny said. "Lay out another sheet," she said. "Come back here."

General Forrest stopped and turned. "Another one?"

"Yes!" Granny said. "A furlough, pass—whatever you busy military establishments call them! So John Sartoris can come home long enough to—" and she said it herself, she looked straight at me and even backed up and said some of it over as though to make sure there wouldn't be any mistake: "—can come back home and give away that damn bride!"

4

And that was all. The day came and Granny waked Ringo and me before sunup and we ate what breakfast we had from two plates on the back steps. And we dug up the trunk and brought it into the house and polished the silver and Ringo and I brought dogwood and red-bud branches from the pasture and Granny cut the flowers, all of them, cutting them herself with Cousin

Melisandre and Philadelphia just carrying the baskets; so many of them until the house was so full that Ringo and I would believe we smelled them even across the pasture each time we came up. Though of course we couldn't—it was just the food—the last ham from the smokehouse and the chickens and the flour which she had been saving along with the bottle of champagne for the day when the North surrendered—which Louvinia had been cooking for two days now, to remind us each time we approached the house of what was going on and that the flowers were there. As if we could have forgotten about the food. And they dressed Cousin Melisandre and, Ringo in his new blue pants and I in my gray ones which were not so new, we stood in the late afternoon on the gallery—Granny and Cousin Melisandre and Louvinia and Philadelphia and Ringo and I— and watched them enter the gate. General Forrest was not one. Ringo and I had thought maybe he might be, if only to bring Cousin Philip. Then we thought that maybe, since Father was coming anyway, General Forrest would let Father bring him, with Cousin Philip maybe handcuffed to Father and the soldier with the bayonet following, or maybe still just handcuffed to the soldier until he and Cousin Melisandre were married and Father unlocked him.

But General Forrest wasn't one, and Cousin Philip wasn't handcuffed to anybody and there was no bayonet and not even a soldier because these were all officers too. And we stood in the parlor while the home-made candles burnt in the last of sunset in the bright candlesticks which Philadelphia and Ringo and I had polished with the rest of the silver because Granny and Louvinia were both busy cooking and even Cousin Melisandre polished a little of it although Louvinia could pick out the ones she polished without hardly looking and hand them to Philadelphia to polish again:—Cousin Melisandre in the dress which hadn't needed to be altered for her at all because Mother wasn't much older than Cousin Melisandre even when she died, and which would still button on Granny too just like it did the day she married in it, and the chaplain and Father and Cousin Philip and the four others in their gray and braid and sabres and Cousin Melisandre's face was all right now and Cousin Philip's was too because it just had the beautiful-girl look on it and none of us had ever seen him look any other way. Then we ate, and Ringo and I anyway had been waiting on that for three days and then we did it and then it was over too, fading just a little each day until the palate no longer remembered and only our mouths would run a little water as we would name the dishes aloud to one another, until even the water would run less and less and less and it would take something we just hoped to eat some day if they ever got done fighting, to make it run at all.

And that was all. The last sound of wheel and hoof died away, Philadelphia came in from the parlor carrying the candlesticks and blowing out the candles as she came, and Louvinia set the kitchen clock on the table and gathered the last of soiled silver from supper into the dishpan and it might never have even been. "Well," Granny said. She didn't move, leaning her forearms on the table a little and we had never seen that before. She spoke to Ringo without turning her head: "Go call Joby and Lucius." And even when we brought the trunk in and set it against the wall and opened back the lid, she didn't move. She didn't even look at Louvinia either. "Put the clock in too," she said. "I don't think we'll bother to time ourselves tonight."

Fish-Hook Gettysburg

STEPHEN VINCENT BENÉT

Two months have passed since Jackson died in the
    woods
And they brought his body back to the Richmond
    State House
To lie there, heaped with flowers, while the bells
    tolled,
Two months of feints and waiting.
                        And now, at length,
The South goes north again in a second raid,
In the last cast for fortune.
                        A two-edged chance
And yet a chance that may burnish a failing star;
For now, on the wide expanse of the Western board,
Strong pieces that fought for the South have been
    swept away
Or penned up in hollow Vicksburg.
                        One cool Spring night
Porter's ironclads run the shore-batteries
Through a velvet stabbed with hot flashes.
                        Grant lands his men,
Drives the relieving force of Johnston away
And sits at last in front of the hollow town
Like a huge brown bear on its haunches, terribly wait-
    ing.
His guns begin to peck at the pillared porches,
The sleepy, sun-spattered streets. His siege has begun.

Forty-eight days that siege and those guns go on

Like a slow hand closing around a hungry throat,
Ever more hungry.
                    The hunger of the hollow towns,
The hunger of sieges, the hunger of lost hope.
As day goes by after day and the shells still whine
Till the town is a great mole-burrow of pits and caves
Where the thin women hide their children, where the
        tired men
Burrow away from the death that falls from the air
And the common sky turned hostile—and still no
        hope,
Still no sight in the sky when the morning breaks
But the brown bear there on his haunches, steadfastly
        waiting,
Waiting like Time for the honey-tree to fall.

The news creeps back to the watchers oversea.
They ponder on it, aloof and irresolute.
The balance they watch is dipping against the South.
It will take great strokes to redress that balance again.
There will be one more moment of shaken scales
When the Laird rams almost alter the scheme of
        things,
But it is distant.
                    The watchers stare at the board
Waiting a surer omen than Chancellorsville
Or any battle won on a Southern ground.

Lee sees that dip of the balance and so prepares
His cast for the surer omen and his last stroke
At the steel-bossed Northern shield. Once before he
        tried
That spear-rush North and was halted. It was a
        chance.
This is a chance. He weighs the chance in his hand

Like a stone, reflecting.
            Four years from Harper's Ferry,
Two years since the First Manassas—and this last year
Stroke after stroke successful—but still no end.

He is a man with a knotty club in his hand
Beating off bulls from the breaks in the pasture fence
And he has beaten them back at each fresh assault,
McClellan—Burnside—Hooker at Chancellorsville—
Pope at the Second Manassas—Banks in the Valley—
But the pasture is trampled; his army needs new pas-
      ture.
An army moves like a locust, eating the grain,
And this grain is well-nigh eaten. He cannot mend
The breaks in his fence with famine or starving hands,
And if he waits the wheel of another year
The bulls will come back full-fed, shaking sharper
      horns
While he faces them empty, armed with a hunger-
      cracked
Unmagic stick.
            There is only this thing to do.
To strike at the shield with the strength that he still
      can use
Hoping to burst it asunder with one stiff blow
And carry the war up North, to the untouched fields
Where his tattered men can feed on the bull's own
      grain,
Get shoes and clothes, take Washington if they can,
Holding the fighting-gauge in any event.
            He weighs
The chance in his hand. I think that he weighed it
      well
And felt a high-tide risen up in his heart
And in his men a high tide.

They were veterans,
They had never been beaten wholly and blocked but
      once,
He had driven four Union armies within a year
And broken three blue commanders from their com-
      mand.
Even now they were fresh from triumph.
                  He cast his stone
Clanging at fortune, and set his fate on the odds.

   2

Lincoln hears the rumor in Washington.
They are moving North.
                  The Pennsylvania cities
Hear it and shake, they are loose, they are moving
      North.
Call up your shotgun-militia, bury your silver,
Shoulder a gun or run away from the State,
They are loose, they are moving.
                  Fighting Joe Hooker has heard it.
He swings his army back across the Potomac,
Rapidly planning, while Lee still visions him South.
Stuart's horse should have brought the news of that
      move
But Stuart is off on a last and luckless raid
Far to the East, and the grey host moves without eyes
Through crucial days.
                  They are in the Cumberland now,
Taking minor towns, feeding fat for a little while,
Pressing horses and shoes, paying out Confederate
      bills
To slow Dutch storekeepers who groan at the money.
They are loose, they are in the North, they are here
      and there.

Halleck rubs his elbows and wonders where,
Lincoln is sleepless, the telegraph-sounders click
In the War Office day and night.
                    There are lies and rumors,
They are only a mile from Philadelphia now,
They are burning York—they are marching on Balti-
        more—

Meanwhile, Lee rides through the heart of the Cum-
        berland.
A great hot sunset colors the marching men,
Colors the horse and the sword and the bearded face
But cannot change that face from its strong repose.
And—miles away—Joe Hooker, by telegraph
Calls for the garrison left at Harper's Ferry
To join him. Elbow-rubbing Halleck refuses.
Hooker resigns command—and fades from the East
To travel West, fight keenly at Lookout Mountain,
Follow Sherman's march as far as Atlanta,
Be ranked by Howard, and tartly resigns once more
Before the end and the fame and the Grand Review,
To die a slow death, in bed, with his fire gone out,
A campfire quenched and forgotten.
                    He deserved
A better and brusquer end that marched with his
        nickname,
This disappointed, hot-tempered, most human man
Who had such faith in himself except for once,
And the once, being Chancellorsville, wiped out the
        rest.
He was often touchy and life was touchy with him,
But the last revenge was a trifle out of proportion.
Such things will happen—Jackson went in his
        strength,
Stuart was riding his horse when the bullet took him,

And Custer died to the trumpet—Dutch Longstreet
    lived
To quarrel and fight dead battles. Lee passed in si-
    lence.
McClellan talked on forever in word and print.
Grant lived to be President. Thomas died sick at heart.

So Hooker goes from our picture—and a spent aide
Reaches Meade's hut at three o'clock in the morning
To wake him with unexpected news of command.

The thin Pennsylvanian puts on his spectacles
To read the order. Tall, sad-faced, and austere,
He has the sharp, long nose of a fighting-bird,
A prudent mouth and a cool, considering mind.
An iron-gray man with none of Hooker's panache,
But resolute and able, well skilled in war;
They call him "the damned old goggle-eyed snapping-
    turtle"
At times, and he does not call out the idol-shout
When he rides his lines, but his prudence is a hard
    prudence,
And can last out storms that break the men with pa-
    nache,
Though it summons no counter-storm when the storm
    is done.

His sombre schoolmaster-eyes read the order well.
It is three days before the battle.
                    He thinks at first
Of a grand review, gives it up, and begins to act.

That morning a spy brings news to Lee in his tent
That the Union army has moved and is on the march.
Lee calls back Ewell and Early from their forays

And summons his host together by the cross-roads
Where Getty came with his ox-cart.
                    So now we see
These two crab-armies fumbling for each other,
As if through a fog of rumor and false report,
These last two days of sleepy, hay-harvest June.
Hot June lying asleep on a shock of wheat
Where the pollen-wind blows over the burnt-gold
        stubble
And the thirsty men march past, stirring thick grey
        dust
From the trodden pikes—till at last, the crab-claws
        touch
At Getty's town, and clutch, and the peaches fall
Cut by the bullets, splashing under the trees.

That meeting was not willed by a human mind,
When we come to sift it.
                    You say a fate rode a horse
Ahead of those lumbering hosts, and in either hand
He carried a skein of omen. And when, at last,
He came to a certain umbrella-copse of trees
That never had heard a cannon or seen dead men,
He knotted the skeins together and flung them down
With a sound like metal.
                    Perhaps. It may have been so.
All that we know is—Meade intended to fight
Some fifteen miles away on the Pipe Creek Line
And where Lee meant to fight him, if forced to fight,
We do not know, but it was not there where they
        fought.
Yet the riding fate,
Blind and deaf and a doom on a lunging horse,
Threw down his skeins and gathered the battle there.

3

Buford came to Gettysburg late that night
Riding West with his brigades of blue horse,
While Pettigrew and his North Carolinians
Were moving East toward the town with a wagon-
        train,
Hoping to capture shoes.
                The two came in touch.
Pettigrew halted and waited for men and orders.
Buford threw out his pickets beyond the town.

The next morning was July first. It was hot and calm.
On the grey side, Heth's division was ready to march
And drive the blue pickets in. There was still no
        thought
Of a planned and decisive battle on either side
Though Buford had seen the strength of those two
        hill-ridges
Soon enough to be famous, and marked one down
As a place to rally if he should be driven back.

He talks with his staff in front of a tavern now.
An officer rides up from the near First Corps.
"What are you doing here, sir?"
                The officer
Explains. He, too, has come there to look for shoes.
—Fabulous shoes of Gettysburg, dead men's shoes,
Did anyone ever wear you, when it was done,
When the men were gone, when the farms were
        spoiled with the bones,
What became of your nails and leather? The swords
        went home,
The swords went into museums and neat glass cases,
The swords look well there. They are clean from the
        war.

You wouldn't put old shoes in a neat glass case,
Still stuck with the mud of marching.
                    And yet, a man
With a taste for such straws and fables, blown by the
          wind,
Might hide a pair in a labelled case sometime
Just to see how the leather looked, set down by the
          swords.

The officer is hardly through with his tale
When Buford orders him back to his command.
"Why, what is the matter, general?"
                    As he speaks
The far-off hollow slam of a single gun
Breaks the warm stillness. The horses prick up their
          ears.
"That's the matter," says Buford and gallops away.

          4

The battle of the first day was a minor battle
As such are counted.
                    That is, it killed many men.
Killed more than died at Bull Run, left thousands
          stricken
With wounds that time might heal for a little while
Or never heal till the breath was out of the flesh.
The First Corps lost half its number in killed and
          wounded.
The pale-faced women, huddled behind drawn blinds
Back in the town, or in apple-cellars, hiding,
Thought it the end of the world, no doubt.
                    And yet,
As the books remark, it was only a minor battle.

There were only two corps engaged on the Union
        side,
Longstreet had not yet come up, nor Ewell's whole
        force,
Hill's corps lacked a division till evening fell.
It was only a minor battle.
                    When the first shot
Clanged out, it was fired from a clump of Union
        vedettes
Holding a farm in the woods beyond the town.
The farmer was there to hear it—and then to see
The troopers scramble back on their restless horses
And go off, firing, as a grey mass came on.
He must have been a peaceable man, that farmer.
It is said that he died of what he had heard and seen
In that one brief moment, although no bullet came
        near him
And the storm passed by and did not burst on his
        farm.
No doubt he was easily frightened. He should have
        reflected
That even minor battles are hardly the place
For peaceable men—but he died instead, it is said.

There were other deaths that day, as of Smiths and
        Clancys,
Otises, Boyds, Virginia and Pennsylvania,
New York, Carolina, Wisconsin, the gathered West,
The tattered Southern marchers dead on the wheat-
        shocks.
Among these deaths a few famous.
                    Reynolds is dead,
The model soldier, gallant and courteous,
Shot from his saddle in the first of the fight.

He was Doubleday's friend, but Doubleday has no
    time
To grieve him, the Union right being driven in
And Heth's Confederates pressing on toward the
    town.
He holds the onrush back till Howard comes up
And takes command for a while.
               The fighting is grim.
Meade has heard the news. He sends Hancock up to
    the field.
Hancock takes command in mid-combat. The grey
    comes on.
Five color-bearers are killed at one Union color,
The last man, dying, still holds up the sagging flag.
The pale-faced women creeping out of their houses,
Plead with retreating bluecoats, "Don't leave us, boys,
Stay with us—hold the town." Their faces are thin,
Their words come tumbling out of a frightened
    mouth.
In a field, far off, a peaceable farmer puts
His hands to his ears, still hearing that one sharp shot
That he will hear and hear till he dies of it.
It is Hill and Ewell now against Hancock and Howard
And a confused, wild clamor—and the high keen
Of the Rebel yell—and the shrill-edged bullet song
Beating down men and grain, while the sweaty fight-
    ers
Grunt as they ram their charges with blackened
    hands.
Till Hancock and Howard are beaten away at last,
Outnumbered and outflanked, clean out of the town,
Retreating as best they can to a fish-hook ridge,
And the clamor dies and the sun is going down
And the tired men think about food.
               The dust-bitten staff

Of Ewell, riding along through the captured streets,
Hear the thud of a bullet striking their general.
Flesh or bone? Death-wound or rub of the game?
"The general's hurt!" They gasp and volley their
    questions.
Ewell turns his head like a bird, "No, I'm not hurt,
    sir,
But, supposing the ball had struck you, General
    Gordon,
We'd have the trouble of carrying you from the field.
You can see how much better fixed for a fight I am.
It don't hurt a mite to be shot in your wooden leg."

So it ends. Lee comes on the field in time to see
The village taken, the Union wave in retreat.
Meade will not reach the ground till one the next
    morning.

So it ends, this lesser battle of the first day,
Starkly disputed and piecemeal won and lost
By corps-commanders who carried no magic plans
Stowed in their sleeves, but fought and held as they
    could.
It is past. The board is staked for the greater game
Which is to follow—The beaten Union brigades
Recoil from the cross-roads town that they tried to
    hold,
And so recoiling, rest on a destined ground.
Who chose that ground?
              There are claimants enough in the books.
Howard thanked by Congress for choosing it
As doubtless, they would have thanked him as well
    had he
Chosen another, once the battle was won,
And there are a dozen ifs on the Southern side,

How, in that first day's evening, if one had known,
If Lee had been there in time, if Jackson had lived,
The heights that cost so much blood in the vain at-
    tempt
To take days later, could have been taken then.
And the ifs and the thanks and the rest are all true
    enough
But we can only say, when we look at the board,
"There it happened. There is the way of the land.
There was the fate, and there the blind swords were
    crossed."

5

Draw a clumsy fish-hook now on a piece of paper,
To the left of the shank, by the bend of the curving
    hook,
Draw a Maltese cross with the top block cut away.
The cross is the town. Nine roads star out from it
East, West, South, North.
                    And now, still more to the left
Of the lopped-off cross, on the other side of the town,
Draw a long, slightly-wavy line of ridges and hills
Roughly parallel to the fish-hook shank.
(The hook of the fish-hook is turned away from the
    cross
And the wavy line.)
                    There your ground and your ridges lie.
The fish-hook is Cemetery Ridge and the North
Waiting to be assaulted—the wavy line
Seminary Ridge whence the Southern assault will
    come.

The valley between is more than a mile in breadth.
It is some three miles from the lowest jut of the cross

To the button at the far end of the fish-hook shank,
Big Round Top, with Little Round Top not far away.
Both ridges are strong and rocky, well made for war.
But the Northern one is the stronger shorter one.
Lee's army must spread out like an uncoiled snake
Lying along a fence-rail, while Meade's can coil
Or half-way coil, like a snake part clung to a stone.
Meade has the more men and the easier shifts to
        make,
Lee the old prestige of triumph and his tried skill.
His task is—to coil his snake round the other snake
Halfway clung to the stone, and shatter it so,
Or to break some point in the shank of the fish-hook
        line
And so cut the snake in two.
                Meade's task is to hold.
That is the chess and the scheme of the wooden
        blocks
Set down on the contour map.
                Having learned so much,
Forget it now, while the ripple lines of the map
Arise into bouldered ridges, tree-grown, bird-visited,
Where the gnats buzz, and the wren builds a hollow
        nest
And the rocks are grey in the sun and black in the
        rain,
And the jacks-in-the-pulpit grow in the cool, damp
        hollows.
See no names of leaders painted upon the blocks
Such as "Hill," or "Hancock," or "Pender"—
                but see instead
Three miles of living men—three long double miles
Of men and guns and horses and fires and wagons,
Teamsters, surgeons, generals, orderlies,
A hundred and sixty thousand living men

Asleep or eating or thinking or writing brief
Notes in the thought of death, shooting dice or swear-
        ing,
Groaning in hospital wagons, standing guard
While the slow stars walk through heaven in silver
        mail,
Hearing a stream or a joke or a horse cropping grass
Or hearing nothing, being too tired to hear.
All night till the round sun comes and the morning
        breaks,
Three double miles of live men.
Listen to them, their breath goes up through the night
In a great chord of life, in the sighing murmur
Of wind-stirred wheat.
                A hundred and sixty thousand
Breathing men, at night, on two hostile ridges set
        down.

                6

The firing began that morning at nine o'clock,
But it was three before the attacks were launched
There were two attacks, one a drive on the Union left
To take the Round Tops, the other one on the right.
Lee had planned them to strike together and, striking
        so,
Cut the Union snake in three pieces.
                It did not happen.
On the left, Dutch Longstreet, slow, pugnacious and
        stubborn,
Hard to beat and just as hard to convince,
Has his own ideas of the battle and does not move
For hours after the hour that Lee had planned,
Though, when he does, he moves with pugnacious
        strength.

Facing him, in the valley before the Round Tops,
Sickles thrusts out blue troops in a weak right angle,
Some distance from the Ridge, by the Emmettsburg
     pike.
There is a peach orchard there, a field of ripe wheat
And other peaceable things soon not to be peaceful.

They say the bluecoats, marching through the ripe
     wheat,
Made a blue-and-yellow picture that men remember
Even now in their age, in their crack-voiced age.
They say the noise was incessant as the sound
Of all wolves howling, when that attack came on.
They say, when the guns all spoke, that the solid
     ground
Of the rocky ridges trembled like a sick child.
We have made the sick earth tremble with other shakings
In our time, in our time, in our time, but it has not taught
     us
To leave the grain in the field.
               So the storm came on
Yelling against the angle.
               The men who fought there
Were the tired fighters, the hammered, the weather-
     beaten,
The very hard-dying men.
               They came and died
And came again and died and stood there and died,
Till at last the angle was crumpled and broken in,
Sickles shot down, Willard, Barlow and Semmes shot
     down,
Wheatfield and orchard bloody and trampled and
     taken,
And Hood's tall Texans sweeping on toward the
     Round Tops

As Hood fell wounded.
                    On Little Round Top's height
Stands a lonely figure, seeing that rush come on—
Greek-mouthed Warren, Meade's chief of engineers.
—Sometimes, and in battle even, a moment comes
When a man with eyes can see a dip in the scales
And, so seeing, reverse a fortune. Warren has eyes
And such a moment comes to him now. He turns
—In a clear flash seeing the crests of the Round Tops
          taken,
The grey artillery there and the battle lost—
And rides off hell-for-leather to gather troops
And bring them up in the very nick of time,
While the grey rush still advances, keening its cry.
The crest is three times taken and then retaken
In fierce wolf-flurries of combat, in gasping Iliads
Too rapid to note or remember, too obscure to freeze
          in a song.
But at last, when the round sun drops, when the nun-
          footed night,
Dark-veiled walker, holding the first weak stars
Like children against her breast, spreads her pure
          cloths there,
The Union still holds the Round Tops and the two
          hard keys of war.

Night falls. The blood drips on the rocks of the
          Devil's Den.
The murmur begins to rise from the thirsty ground
Where the twenty thousand dead and wounded lie.
Such was Longstreet's war, and such was the Union
          defence,
The deaths and the woundings, the victory and defeat
At the end of the fish-hook shank.
                    And so Longstreet failed

Ere Ewell and Early struck the fish-hook itself
At Culp's Hill and the Ridge and at Cemetery Hill,
With better fortune, though not with fortune enough
To plant hard triumph deep on the sharp-edged rocks
And break the scales of the snake. . . .

Thus ended the second day of the locked bull-horns
And the wounding or slaying of the twenty thousand.
And thus night came to cover it.
                    So the field
Was alive all night with whispers and words and
          sighs,
So the slow blood dripped in the rocks of the Devil's
          Den.
Lincoln, back in his White House, asks for news.
The War Department has little. There are reports
Of heavy firing near Gettysburg—that is all.
Davis, in Richmond, knows as little as he.
In hollow Vicksburg, the shells come down and come
          down
And the end is but two days off.
                    On the field itself
Meade calls a council and considers retreat.
His left has held and the Round Tops still are his.
But his right has been shaken, his centre pierced for a
          time,
The enemy holds part of his works on Culp's Hill,
His losses have been most stark.
                    He thinks of these things
And decides at last to fight it out where he stands.

          7

Another clear dawn breaks over Gettysburg,
Promising heat and fair weather—and with the dawn

The guns are crashing again.
                    It is the third day.
The morning wears with a stubborn fight at Culp's
        Hill
That ends at last in Confederate repulse
And that barb-end of the fish-hook cleared of the
        grey.

Lee has tried his strokes on the right and left of the
        line.
The centre remains—that centre yesterday pierced
For a brief, wild moment in Wilcox's attack,
But since then trenched, reinforced and alive with
        guns.
It is a chance. All war is a chance like that.
Lee considers the chance and the force he has left to
        spend
And states his will.
                    Dutch Longstreet, the independent,
Demurs, as he has demurred since the fight began.
He had disapproved of this battle from the first
And that disapproval had added and is to add
Another weight in the balance against the grey.
It is not our task to try him for sense or folly,
Such men are the men they are—but an hour comes
Sometimes, to fix such men in most fateful parts,
As now with Longstreet who, if he had his orders
As they were given, neither obeyed them quite
Nor quite refused them, but acted as he thought best,
So did the half-thing, failed as he thought he would,
Felt justified and wrote all of his reasons down
Later in controversy.
                    We do not need
Such controversies to see that pugnacious man
Talking to Lee, a stubborn line in his brow

And that unseen fate between them.
>> Lee hears him out
Unmoved, unchanging.
>> "The enemy is there
And I am going to strike him," says Lee, inflexibly.

8

At one o'clock the first signal-gun was fired
And the solid ground began to be sick anew.
For two hours then that sickness, the unhushed roar
Of two hundred and fifty cannon firing like one.

By Philadelphia, eighty-odd miles away,
An old man stooped and put his ear to the ground
And heard that roar, it is said, like the vague sea-
>> clash
In a hollow conch-shell, there, in his flowerbeds.
He had planted trumpet-flowers for fifteen years
But now the flowers were blowing an iron noise
Through earth itself. He wiped his face on his sleeve
And tottered back to his house with fear in his eyes.

The caissons began to blow up in the Union
>> batteries. . . .

The cannonade fell still. All along the fish-hook line,
The tired men stared at the smoke and waited for it to
>> clear;
The men in the centre waited, their rifles gripped in
>> their hands,
By the trees of the riding fate, and the low stone wall,
>> and the guns.

These were Hancock's men, the men of the Second
   Corps,
Eleven States were mixed there, where Minnesota
   stood
In battle-order with Maine, and Rhode Island beside
   New York,
The metals of all the North, cooled into an axe of war.

The strong sticks of the North, bound into a fasces-
   shape,
The hard winters of snow, the wind with the cutting
   edge,
And against them came that summer that does not die
   with the year,
Magnolia and honeysuckle and the blue Virginia flag.

Tall Pickett went up to Longstreet—his handsome face
   was drawn.
George Pickett, old friend of Lincoln's in days gone
   by with the blast,
When he was a courteous youth and Lincoln the
   strange shawled man
Who would talk in a Springfield street with a boy
   who dreamt of a sword.

Dreamt of a martial sword, as swords are martial in
   dreams,
And the courtesy to use it, in the old bright way of
   the tales.
Those days are gone with the blast. He has his sword
   in his hand.
And he will use it today, and remember that using
   long.

He came to Longstreet for orders, but Longstreet
    would not speak.
He saw Old Peter's mouth and the thought in Old
    Peter's mind.
He knew the task that was set and the men that he
    had to lead
And a pride came into his face while Longstreet stood
    there dumb.

"I shall go forward, sir," he said, and turned to his
    men.
The commands went down the line. The grey ranks
    started to move.
Slowly at first, then faster, in order, stepping like
    deer,
The Virginians, the fifteen thousand, the seventh wave
    of the tide.

There was a death-torn mile of broken ground to
    cross,
And a low stone wall at the end, and behind it the
    Second Corps,
And behind that force another, fresh men who had
    not yet fought.
They started to cross that ground. The guns began to
    tear them.

From the hill they say it seemed more like a sea than
    a wave,
A sea continually torn by stones flung out of the sky,
And yet, as it came, still closing, closing and rolling
    on,
As the moving sea closes over the flaws and rips of
    the tide.

You could mark the path that they took by the dead
    that they left behind,
Spilled from that deadly march as a cart spills meal
    on a road,
And yet they came on unceasing, the fifteen thousand
    no more,
And the blue Virginia flag did not fall, did not fall,
    did not fall.

They halted but once to fire as they came. Then the
    smoke closed down
And you could not see them, and then, as it cleared
    again for a breath,
They were coming still but divided, gnawed at by
    blue attacks,
One flank half-severed and halted, but the centre still
    like a tide.

Cushing ran down the last of his guns to the battle-
    line.
The rest had been smashed to scrap by Lee's artillery
    fire.
He held his guts in his hand as the charge came up to
    the wall
And his guns spoke out for him once before he fell to
    the ground.

Armistead leapt the wall and laid his hand on the
    gun,
The last of the three brigadiers who ordered Pickett's
    brigades,
He waved his hat on his sword and "Give 'em the
    steel!" he cried,
A few men followed him over. The rest were beaten
    or dead.

A few men followed him over. There had been fifteen
    thousand
When that sea began its march toward the fish-hook
    ridge and the wall.
So they came on in strength, light-footed, stepping
    like deer,
So they died or were taken. So the iron entered their
    flesh.

Lee, a mile away, in the shade of a little wood,
Stared, with his mouth shut down, and saw them go
    and be slain,
And then saw for a single moment, the blue Virginia
    flag
Planted beyond the wall, by that other flag that he
    knew.

The two flags planted together, one instant, like hos-
    tile flowers.
Then the smoke wrapped both in a mantle—and
    when it had blown away,
Armistead lay in his blood, and the rest were dead or
    down,
And the valley grey with the fallen and the wreck of
    the broken wave.

Pickett gazed around him, the boy who had dreamt of
    a sword
And talked with a man named Lincoln. The sword
    was still in his hand.
He had gone out with fifteen thousand. He came back
    to his lines with five.
He fought well till the war was over, but a thing was
    cracked in his heart.

9

The night of the third day falls. The battle is done.
Lee entrenches that night upon Seminary Ridge.
All next day the battered armies still face each other
Like enchanted beasts.
                Lee thinks he may be attacked,
Hopes for it, perhaps, is not, and prepares his retreat.

Vicksburg has fallen, hollow Vicksburg has fallen,
The cavedwellers creep from their caves and blink at
      the sun.
The pan of the Southern balance goes down and
      down.
The cotton is withering.

Army of Northern Virginia, haggard and tattered,
Tramping back on the pikes, through the dust-white
      summer,
With your wounds still fresh, your burden of prison-
      ers,
Your burden of sick and wounded,
"One long groan of human anguish six miles long."
You reach the swollen Potomac at long last,
A foe behind, a risen river in front,
And fording that swollen river, in the dim starlight,
In the yellow and early dawn,
Still have heart enough for the tall, long-striding
      soldiers
To mock the short, half swept away by the stream.
"Better change your name to Lee's Waders, boys!"
"Come on you shorty—get a ride on my back."
"Aw, it's just we ain't had a bath in seven years
And General Lee, he knows we need a good bath."

So you splash and slip through the water and come at
        last
Safe, to the Southern side, while Meade does not
        strike;
Safe to take other roads, safe to march upon roads
        you know
For two long years. And yet—each road that you take,
Each dusty road leads to Appomattox now.

The Burning

EUDORA WELTY

Delilah was dancing up to the front with a message; that was how she happened to be the one to see. A horse was coming in the house, by the front door. The door had been shoved wide open. And all behind the horse, a crowd with a long tail of dust was coming after, all the way up their road from the gate between the cedar trees.

She ran on into the parlor, where they were. They were standing up before the fireplace, their white sewing dropped over their feet, their backs turned, both ladies. Miss Theo had eyes in the back of her head.

"Back you go, Delilah," she said.

"It ain't me, it's them," cried Delilah, and now there were running feet to answer all over the downstairs; Ophelia and all had heard. Outside the dogs were thundering. Miss Theo and Miss Myra, keeping their backs turned to whatever shape or ghost Commotion would take when it came—as long as it was still in the yard, mounting the steps, crossing the porch, or even, with a smell of animal sudden as the smell of snake, planting itself in the front hall—they still had to see it if it came in the parlor, the white horse. It drew up just over the ledge of the double doors Delilah had pushed open, and the ladies lifted their heads together and looked in the mirror over the fireplace, the one called the Venetian mirror, and there it was.

It was a white silhouette, like something cut out of the room's dark. July was so bright outside, and the parlor so dark for coolness, that at first nobody but Delilah could see. Then Miss Myra's racing speech interrupted everything.

"Will you take me on the horse? Please take me first."

It was a towering, sweating, grimacing, uneasy white horse. It had brought in two soldiers with red eyes and clawed, mosquito-racked faces—one a rider, hang-jawed and head-hanging, and the other walking by its side, all breathing in here now as loud as trumpets.

Miss Theo with shut eyes spoke just behind Miss Myra. "Delilah, what is it you came in your dirty apron to tell me?"

The sisters turned with linked hands and faced the room.

"Come to tell you we got the eggs away from black broody hen and sure enough, they's addled," said Delilah.

She saw the blue rider drop his jaw still lower. That was his laugh. But the other soldier set his boot on the carpet and heard the creak in the floor. As if reminded by tell-tale, he took another step, and with his red eyes sticking out he went as far as Miss Myra and took her around that little bending waist. Before he knew it, he had her lifted as high as a child, she was so light. The other soldier with a grunt came down from the horse's back and went toward Miss Theo.

"Step back. Delilah, out of harm's way," said Miss Theo, in such a company-voice that Delilah thought harm was one of two men.

"Hold my horse, nigger," said the man it was.

Delilah took the bridle as if she'd always done that, and held the horse that loomed there in the mirror—she could see it there now, herself—while more blurred and

blind-like in the room between it and the door the first
soldier shoved the tables and chairs out of the way behind Miss Myra, who flitted when she ran, and pushed
her down where she stood and dropped on top of her.
There in the mirror the parlor remained, filled up with
dusted pictures, and shuttered since six o'clock against
the heat and that smell of smoke they were all so tired
of, still glimmering with precious, breakable things
white ladies were never tired of and never broke, unless
they were mad at each other. Behind *her*, the bare yawn
of the hall was at her back, and the front stair's shadow,
big as a tree and empty. Nobody went up there without
being seen, and nobody was supposed to come down.
Only if a cup or a silver spoon or a little string of spools
on a blue ribbon came hopping down the steps like a
frog, sometimes Delilah was the one to pick it up and
run back up with it. Outside the mirror's frame, the flat
of Miss Theo's hand came down on mankind with a
boisterous sound.

Then Miss Theo lifted Miss Myra without speaking
to her; Miss Myra closed her eyes but was not asleep.
Her bands of black hair awry, her clothes rustling stiffly
as clothes through winter quiet, Miss Theo strode half-
carrying Miss Myra to the chair in the mirror, and put
her down. It was the red, rubbed velvet, pretty chair
like Miss Myra's ringbox. Miss Myra threw her head
back, face up to the little plaster flowers going around
the ceiling. She was asleep somewhere, if not in her
eyes.

One of the men's voices spoke out, all gone with
righteousness. "We just come in to inspect."

"You presume, you dare," said Miss Theo. Her
hand came down to stroke Miss Myra's back-flung head
in a strong, forbidding rhythm. From upstairs, Phinny
threw down his breakfast plate, but Delilah did not

move. Miss Myra's hair streamed loose behind her, bright gold, with the combs caught like leaves in it. Maybe it was to keep her like this, asleep in the heart, that Miss Theo stroked her on and on, too hard.

"It's orders to inspect beforehand," said the soldier.

"Then inspect," said Miss Theo. "No one in the house to prevent it. Brother—no word. Father—dead. Mercifully so—" She spoke in an almost rough-and-rumble kind of way used by ladies who didn't like company—never did like company, for anybody.

Phinny threw down his cup. The horse, shivering, nudged Delilah who was holding him there, a good obedient slave in her fresh-ironed candy-stripe dress beneath her black apron. She would have had her turban tied on, had she known all this ahead, like Miss Theo. "Never is Phinny away. Phinny here. He a he," she said.

Miss Myra's face was turned up as if she were dead, or as if she were a fierce and hungry little bird. Miss Theo rested her hand for a moment in the air above her head.

"Is it shame that's stopping your inspection?" Miss Theo asked. "I'm afraid you found the ladies of this house a trifle out of your element. My sister's the more delicate one, as you see. May I offer you this young kitchen Negro, as I've always understood—"

That Northerner gave Miss Theo a serious, recording look as though she had given away what day the mail came in.

"My poor little sister," Miss Theo went on to Miss Myra, "don't mind what you hear. Don't mind this old world." But Miss Myra knocked back the stroking hand. Kitty came picking her way into the room and sat between the horse's front feet; Friendly was her name.

One soldier rolled his head toward the other. "What was you saying to me when we come in, Virge?"

"I was saying I opined they wasn't gone yet."

"*Wasn't* they?"

Suddenly both of them laughed, jolting each other so hard that for a second it looked like a fight. Then one said with straight face, "We come with orders to set the house afire, ma'am," and the other one said, "General Sherman."

"I hear you."

"Don't you think we're going to do it? We done just burnt up Jackson twice," said the first soldier with his eye on Miss Myra. His voice made a man's big echo in the hall, like a long time ago. The horse whinnied and moved his head and feet.

"Like I was telling you, you ladies ought to been out. You didn't get no word here we was coming?" The other soldier pointed one finger at Miss Theo. She shut her eyes.

"Lady, they told you." Miss Myra's soldier looked hard at Miss Myra there. "And when your own people tell you something's coming to burn your house down, the business-like thing to do is get out of the way. And the right thing. I ain't beholden to tell you no more times now."

"Then go."

"Burning up *people's* further'n I go yet."

Miss Theo stared him down. "I see no degree."

So it was Miss Myra's soldier that jerked Delilah's hand from the bridle and turned her around, and cursed the Bedlam-like horse which began to beat the hall floor behind. Delilah listened, but Phinny did not throw anything more down; maybe he had crept to the landing, and now looked over. He was scared, if not of horses, then of men. He didn't know anything about them. The horse did get loose; he took a clattering trip through the hall and dining room and library, until at last his rider caught him. Then Delilah was set on his back.

She looked back over her shoulder through the doorway, and saw Miss Theo shake Miss Myra and catch the peaked face with its purple eyes and slap it.

"Myra," she said, "collect your senses. We have to go out in front of them."

Miss Myra slowly lifted her white arm, like a lady who has been asked to dance, and called, "Delilah!" Because that was the one she saw being lifted onto the horse's hilly back and ridden off through the front door. Skittering among the iron shoes, Kitty came after, trotting fast as a little horse herself, and ran ahead to the woods, where she was never seen again; but Delilah, from where she was set up on the horse and then dragged down on the grass, never called after her.

She might have been saving her breath for the screams that soon took over the outdoors and circled that house they were going to finish for sure now. She screamed, young and strong, for them all—for everybody that wanted her to scream for them, for everybody that didn't; and sometimes it seemed to her that she was screaming her loudest for Delilah, who was lost now—carried out of the house, not knowing how to get back.

Still inside, the ladies kept them waiting.

Miss Theo finally brought Miss Myra out through that wide-open front door and across the porch with the still perfect and motionless vine shadows. There were some catcalls and owl hoots from under the trees.

"Now hold back, boys. They's too ladylike for you."

"Ladies must needs take their time."

"And then they're no damn good at it!" came a clear, youthful voice, and under the branches somewhere a banjo was stroked to call up the campfires further on, later in the evening, when all this would be over and done.

The sisters showed no surprise to see soldiers and Negroes alike (old Ophelia in the way, talking, talking) strike into and out of the doors of the house, the front now the same as the back, to carry off beds, tables, candlesticks, washstands, cedar buckets, china pitchers, with their backs bent double; or the horses ready to go; or the food of the kitchen bolted down—and so much of it thrown away, this must be a second dinner; or the unsilenceable dogs, the old pack mixed with the strangers and fighting with all their hearts over bones. The last skinny sacks were thrown on the wagons—the last flour, the last scraping and clearing from Ophelia's shelves, even her pepper-grinder. The silver Delilah could count was counted on strange blankets and then, knocking against the teapot, rolled together, tied up like a bag of bones. A drummer boy with his drum around his neck caught both Miss Theo's peacocks, Marco and Polo, and wrung their necks in the yard. Nobody could look at those bird-corpses; nobody did.

The sisters left the porch like one, and in step, hands linked, came through the high grass in their crushed and only dresses, and walked under the trees. They came to a stop as if it was moonlight under the leafy frame of the big tree with the swing, without any despising left in their faces which were the same as one, as one face that didn't belong to anybody. This one clarified face, looking both left and right, could make out every one of those men through the bushes and tree trunks, and mark every looting slave also, as all stood momently fixed like serenaders by the light of a moon.

Only old Ophelia was talking all the time, all the time, telling everybody in her own way about the trouble here, but of course nobody could understand a thing that day anywhere in the world.

"What are they fixing to do now, Theo?" asked Miss Myra, with a frown about to burn into her too-white forehead.

"What they want to," Miss Theo said, folding her arms.

To Delilah that house they were carrying the torches to was like one just now coming into being— like the showboat that slowly came through the trees just once in her time, at the peak of high water—bursting with the unknown, sparking in ruddy light, with a minute to go before that ear-aching cry of the calliope.

When it came—but it was a bellowing like a bull, that came from inside—Delilah drew close, with Miss Theo's skirt to peep around, and Miss Theo's face looked down like death itself and said, "Remember this. You black monkeys," as the blaze outdid them all.

A while after the burning, when everybody had gone away, Miss Theo and Miss Myra, finding and taking hold of Delilah, who was face-down in a ditch with her eyes scorched open, did at last go beyond the tramped-down gate and away through the grand worthless fields they themselves had had burned long before.

It was a hot afternoon, hot out here in the open, and it played a trick on them with a smell and prophecy of fall—it was the burning. The brown wet standing among the stumps in the cracked cup of the pond tasted as hot as coffee and as bitter. There was still and always smoke between them and the sun.

After all the July miles, there Jackson stood, burned

twice, or who knew if it was a hundred times, facing them in the road. Delilah could see through Jackson like a haunt, it was all chimneys, all scooped out. There were soldiers with guns among the ashes, but these ashes were cold. Soon even these two ladies, who had been everywhere and once knew their way, told each other they were lost. While some soldiers looked them over, they pointed at what they couldn't see, traced gone-away spires, while a horse without his rider passed brushing his side against them and ran down a black alley softly, and did not return.

They walked here and there, sometimes over the same track, holding hands all three, like the timeless time it snowed, and white and black went to play together in hushed woods. They turned loose only to point and name.

"The State House."—"The school."

"The Blind School."—"The penitentiary!"

"The big stable."—"The Deaf-and-Dumb."

"Oh! Remember when we passed three of *them*, sitting on a hill?" They went on matching each other, naming and claiming ruin for ruin.

"The lunatic asylum!"—"The State House."

"No, I said that. Now where are we? That's surely Captain Jack Calloway's hitching post."

"But why would the hitching post be standing and the rest not?"

"And ours not."

"I think I should have told you, Myra—"

"Tell me now."

"Word *was* sent to us to get out when it was sent to the rest on Vicksburg Road. Two days' warning. I believe it was a message from General Pemberton."

"Don't worry about it now. Oh no, of course we

couldn't leave," said Miss Myra. A soldier watched her in the distance, and she recited:

> *"There was a man in our town*
> *And he was wondrous wise.*
> *He jumped into a bramble bush*
> *And scratched out both his eyes."*

She stopped, looking at the soldier.

"He sent word." Miss Theo went on, "General Pemberton sent word, for us all to get out ahead of what was coming. You were in the summerhouse when it came. It was two days' warning—but I couldn't bring myself to call and tell you, Myra. I suppose I couldn't convince myself—couldn't quite *believe* that they meant to come and visit that destruction on us."

"Poor Theo. I could have."

"No you couldn't. I couldn't *understand* that message, any more than Delilah here could have. I can reproach myself now, of course, with everything." And they began to walk boldly through and boldly out of the burnt town, single file.

"Not everything, Theo. Who had Phinny? Remember?" cried Miss Myra ardently.

"Hush."

"If I hadn't had Phinny, that would've made it all right. Then Phinny wouldn't have—"

"Hush, dearest, that wasn't *your* baby, you know. It was Brother Benton's baby. I won't have your nonsense now." Miss Theo led the way through the ashes, marching in front. Delilah was in danger of getting left behind.

"—perished. Dear Benton. So good. Nobody else would have felt so *bound*," Miss Myra said.

"Not after I told him what he owed a little life!

Each little life is a *man's* fault. I said that. Oh, who'll ever forget that awful day?"

"Benton's forgotten, if he's dead. He was so good after that too, never married."

"Stayed home, took care of his sisters. Only wanted to be forgiven."

"There has to be somebody to take care of everybody."

"I told him, he must never dream he was *inflicting* his sisters. That's what we're for."

"And it never would have inflicted us. We could have lived and died. Until *they* came."

"In at the front door on the back of a horse," said Miss Theo. "If Benton had been there!"

"I'll never know what possessed them, riding in like that," said Miss Myra almost mischievously; and Miss Theo turned.

"And *you said*—"

"I said something wrong," said Miss Myra quickly. "I apologize, Theo."

"No, I blame only myself. That I let you remain one hour in that house after it was doomed. I thought I was equal to it, and I proved I was, but not you."

"Oh, to my shame you saw me, dear! Why do you say it wasn't my baby?"

"Now don't start that nonsense over again," said Miss Theo, going around a hole.

"I had Phinny. When we were all at home and happy together. Are you going to take Phinny away from me now?"

Miss Theo pressed her cheeks with her palms and showed her pressed, pensive smile as she looked back over her shoulder.

Miss Myra said, "Oh, don't *I* know who it really belonged to, who it loved the best, that baby?"

"I won't have you misrepresenting yourself."

"It's never what I intended."

"Then reason dictates you hush."

Both ladies sighed, and so did Delilah; they were so tired of going on. Miss Theo still walked in front but she was looking behind her through the eyes in the back of her head.

"You hide him if you want to," said Miss Myra. "Let Papa shut up all upstairs. I had him, dear. It was an officer, no, one of our beaux that used to come out and hunt with Benton. It's because I was always the impetuous one, highstrung and so easily carried away. . . . And if Phinny *was* mine—"

"Don't you know he's black?" Miss Theo blocked the path.

"He *was* white." Then, "He's black *now*," whispered Miss Myra, darting forward and taking her sister's hands. Their shoulders were pressed together, as if they were laughing or waiting for something more to fall.

"If I only had something to eat!" sobbed Miss Myra, and once more let herself be embraced. One eye showed over the tall shoulder. "Oh, Delilah!"

"Could be he got out," called Delilah in a high voice. "He strong, he."

"Who?"

"Could be Phinny's out loose. Don't cry."

"Look yonder. What do I see? I see the Dicksons' perfectly good hammock still under the old pecan trees," Miss Theo said to Miss Myra, and spread her hand.

There was some little round silver cup, familiar to the ladies, in the hammock when they came to it down in the grove. Lying on its side with a few drops in it, it made them smile.

The yard was charged with butterflies. Miss Myra, as if she could wait no longer, climbed into the hammock and lay down with ankles crossed. She took up the cup like a story book she'd begun and left there yesterday, holding it before her eyes in those freckling fingers, slowly picking out the ants.

"So still out here and all," Miss Myra said. "Such a big sky. Can you get used to that? And all the figs dried up. I wish it would rain."

"Won't rain till Saturday," said Delilah.

"Delilah, don't go 'way."

"Don't you try, Delilah," said Miss Theo.

"No'm."

Miss Theo sat down, rested a while, though she did not know how to sit on the ground and was afraid of grasshoppers, and then she stood up, shook out her skirt, and cried out to Delilah, who had backed off far to one side, where some chickens were running around loose with nobody to catch them.

"Come back here, Delilah! Too late for that!" She said to Miss Myra, "The Lord will provide. We've still got Delilah, and as long as we've got her we'll use her, my dearie."

Miss Myra "let the cat die" in the hammock. Then she gave her hand to climb out, Miss Theo helped her, and without needing any help for herself Miss Theo untied the hammock from the pecan trees. She was long bent over it, and Miss Myra studied the butterflies. She had left the cup sitting on the ground in the shade of the tree. At last Miss Theo held up two lengths of cotton rope, the red and the white strands untwisted from each other, bent like the hair of ladies taken out of plaits in the morning.

Delilah, given the signal, darted up the tree and hooking her toes made the ropes fast to the two branches a sociable distance apart, where Miss Theo pointed. When she slid down, she stood waiting while they settled it, until Miss Myra repeated enough times, in a spoiled sweet way, "I bid to be first." It was what Miss Theo wanted all the time. Then Delilah had to squat and make a basket with her fingers, and Miss Myra tucked up her skirts and stepped her ashy shoe in the black hands.

"Tuck under, Delilah."

Miss Myra, who had ordered that, stepped over Delilah's head and stood on her back, and Delilah felt her presence tugging there as intimately as a fish's on a line, each longing Miss Myra had to draw away from Miss Theo, draw away from Delilah, away from that tree.

Delilah rolled her eyes around. The noose was being tied by Miss Theo's puckered hands like a bonnet on a windy day, and Miss Myra's young, lifted face was looking out.

"I learned as a child how to tie, from a picture book in Papa's library—not that I ever was called on," Miss Theo said. "I guess I was always something of a tomboy." She kissed Miss Myra's hand and at almost the same instant Delilah was seized by the ribs and dragged giggling backward, out from under—not soon enough, for Miss Myra kicked her in the head—a bad kick, almost as if that were Miss Theo or a man up in the tree, who meant what he was doing.

Miss Theo stood holding Delilah and looking up—helping herself to grief. No wonder Miss Myra used to hide in the summerhouse with her reading, screaming sometimes when there was nothing but Delilah throwing the dishwater out on the ground.

"I've proved," said Miss Theo to Delilah, dragging her by more than main force back to the tree, "what I've always suspicioned: that I'm brave as a lion. That's right: look at me. If I ordered you back up that tree to help my sister down to the grass and shade, you'd turn and run: I know your minds. You'd desert me with your work half done. So I haven't said a word about it. About mercy. As soon as you're through, you can go, and leave us where you've put us, unspared, just alike. And that's the way they'll find us. The sight will be good for them for what they've done," and she pushed Delilah down and walked up on her shoulders, weighting her down like a rock.

Miss Theo looped her own knot up there; there was no mirror or sister to guide her. Yet she was quicker this time than last time, but Delilah was quicker too. She rolled over in a ball, and then she was up running, look-ing backward, crying. Behind her Miss Theo came sail-ing down from the tree. She was always too powerful for a lady. Even those hens went flying up with a shriek, as if they felt her shadow on their backs. Now she reached in the grass.

There was nothing for Delilah to do but hide, down in the jungly grass choked with bitterweed and black-eyed susans, wild to the pricking skin, with many heads nodding, cauldrons of ants, with butterflies riding them, grasshoppers hopping them, mosquitoes making the air alive, down in the loud and lonesome grass that was rank enough almost to matt the sky over. Once, stung all over and wild to her hair's ends, she ran back and asked Miss Theo, "What must I do now? Where must I go?" But Miss Theo, whose eyes from the ground were looking straight up at her, wouldn't tell. Delilah danced away from her, back to her distance, and crouched down. She believed Miss Theo twisted in the grass like

a dead snake until the sun went down. She herself held
still like a mantis until the grass had folded and spread
apart at the falling of dew. This was after the chickens
had gone to roost in a strange uneasy tree against the
cloud where the guns still boomed and the way from
Vicksburg was red. Then Delilah could find her feet.

She knew where Miss Theo was. She could see the
last white of Miss Myra, the stockings. Later, down by
the swamp, in a wading bird tucked in its wing for
sleep, she saw Miss Myra's ghost.

After being lost a day and a night or more, crouching awhile, stealing awhile through the solitudes of
briar bushes, she came again to Rose Hill. She knew it
by the chimneys and by the crape myrtle off to the side,
where the bottom of the summerhouse stood empty as
an egg basket. Some of the flowers looked tasty, like
chicken legs fried a little black.

Going around the house, climbing over the barrier
of the stepless back doorsill, and wading into ashes, she
was lost still, inside that house. She found an iron pot
and a man's long boot, a doorknob and a little book
fluttering, its leaves spotted and fluffed like guinea
feathers. She took up the book and read out from it,
"Ba-ba-ba-ba-ba—trash." She was being Miss Theo taking away Miss Myra's reading. Then she saw the Venetian mirror down in the chimney's craw, flat and face-
up in the cinders.

Behind her the one standing wall of the house held
notched and listening like the big ear of King Solomon
into which poured the repeated asking of birds. The tree
stood and flowered. What must she do? Crouching suddenly to the ground, she heard the solid cannon, the
galloping, the low fast drum of burning. Crawling on
her knees she went to the glass and rubbed it with spit

and leaned over it and saw a face all neck and ears, then
gone. Before it she opened and spread her arms; she
had seen Miss Myra do that, try that. But its gleam was
addled.

Though the mirror did not know Delilah, Delilah
would have known that mirror anywhere, because it
was set between black men. Their arms were raised to
hold up the mirror's roof, which now the swollen mirror brimmed, among gold leaves and gold heads—black
men dressed in gold, looking almost into the glass
themselves, as if to look back through a door, men now
half-split away, flattened with fire, bearded, noseless as
the moss that hung from swamp trees.

Where the mirror did not cloud like the horse-tram-
pled spring, gold gathered itself from the winding water, and honey under water started to flow, and then the
gold fields were there, hardening gold. Through the water, gold and honey twisted up into houses, trembling.
She saw people walking the bridges in early light with
hives of houses on their heads, men in dresses, some
with red birds; and monkeys in velvet; and ladies with
masks laid over their faces looking from pointed windows. Delilah supposed that was Jackson before Sherman came. Then it was gone. In this noon quiet, here
where all had passed by, unless indeed it had gone in,
she waited on her knees.

The mirror's cloudy bottom sent up minnows of
light to the brim where now a face pure as a water-lily
shadow was floating. Almost too small and deep down
to see, they were quivering, leaping to life, fighting, ap-
ing old things Delilah had seen done in this world already, sometimes what men had done to Miss Theo and
Miss Myra and the peacocks and to slaves, and sometimes what a slave had done and what anybody now
could do to anybody. Under the flicker of the sun's

licks, then under its whole blow and blare, like an un-
heard scream, like an act of mercy gone, as the wall-less
light and July blaze struck through from the opened
sky, the mirror felled her flat.

She put her arms over her head and waited, for
they would all be coming again, gathering under her
and above her, bees saddled like horses out of the air,
butterflies harnessed to one another, bats with masks
on, birds together, all with their weapons bared. She listened for the blows, and dreaded that whole army of
wings—of flies, birds, serpents, their glowing enemy
faces and bright kings' dresses, that banner of colors
forked out, all this world that was flying, striking,
stricken, falling, gilded or blackened, mortally splitting
and falling apart, proud turbans unwinding, turning
like the spotted dying leaves of fall, spiraling down to
bottomless ash; she dreaded the fury of all the butterflies and dragonflies in the world riding, blades uncon-
cealed and at point—descending, and rising again from
the waters below, down under, one whale made of his
own grave, opening his mouth to swallow Jonah one
more time.

Jonah!—a homely face to her, that could still look
back from the red lane he'd gone down, even if it was
too late to speak. He was her Jonah, her Phinny, her
black monkey; she worshiped him still, though it was
long ago he was taken from her the first time.

Stiffly, Delilah got to her feet. She cocked her head,
looked sharp into the mirror, and caught the motherly
image—head wagging in the flayed forehead of a horse
with ears and crest up stiff, the shield and the drum of
big swamp birdskins, the horns of deer sharpened to cut
and kill with. She showed her teeth. Then she looked in
the feathery ashes and found Phinny's bones. She

ripped a square from her manifold fullness of skirts and tied up the bones in it.

She set foot in the road then, walking stilted in Miss Myra's shoes and carrying Miss Theo's shoes tied together around her neck, her train in the road behind her. She wore Miss Myra's willing rings—had filled up two fingers—but she had had at last to give up the puzzle of Miss Theo's bracelet with the chain. They were two stones now, scalding-white. When the combs were being lifted from her hair, Miss Myra had come down too, beside her sister.

Light on Delilah's head the Jubilee cup was set. She paused now and then to lick the rim and taste again the ghost of sweet that could still make her tongue start clinging—some sweet lapped up greedily long ago, only a mystery now when or who by. She carried her own black locust stick to drive the snakes.

Following the smell of horses and fire, to men, she kept in the wheel tracks till they broke down at the river. In the shade underneath the burned and fallen bridge she sat on a stump and chewed for a while, without dreams, the comb of a dirtdauber. Then once more kneeling, she took a drink from the Big Black, and pulled the shoes off her feet and waded in.

Submerged to the waist, to the breast, stretching her throat like a sunflower stalk above the river's opaque skin, she kept on, her treasure stacked on the roof of her head, hands laced upon it. She had forgotten how or when she knew, and she did not know what day this was, but she knew—it would not rain, the river would not rise, until Saturday.

Pillar of Fire

SHELBY FOOTE

Ankle deep in the dusty places, the road led twelve miles from the landing, around the head of a horseshoe lake and down its eastern slope where the houses were. We left the gunboat at eight oclock in brilliant sunlight, two mounted officers wearing sabers and sashes and thirty Negro infantrymen in neat blue uniforms; at noon the colonel halted the column before a two-story frame structure with a brick portico and squat, whitewashed pillars. He sat a hammer-headed roan, an early-middle-aged man with a patch across one eye.

"Looks old," he said, rolling his cigar along his lower lip. He faced front, addressing the house itself. "Ought to burn pretty," he added after a pause, perhaps to explain why he had not chosen one of the larger ones in both directions. I saw that he was smiling, and that was as usual at such a time, the head lifted to expose the mouth beneath the wide pepper-and-salt mustache. Behind us the troops were quiet: so quiet that when the colonel turned in the saddle, leather squeaked. "Walk up there, Mr. Lundy, and give them the news."

The troops stood at ease in a column of fours, the rifle barrels slanting and glinting. Above their tunics, which were powdered with dust except where they were splotched a darker blue at backs and armpits from four hours of hard marching, their faces appeared cracked as if by erosion where sweat had run.

"Orderly," I said. A soldier stepped out of ranks

and held the reins near the snaffle while I dismounted on the off side, favoring my stiff right leg. I went up toward the house. When the colonel called after me, something I could not distinguish above the sound of my boots crunching gravel on the driveway, I halted and faced about. "Sir?"

"Tell them twenty minutes!" With one arm he made the sweeping gesture I had come to know so well. "To clear out!" I heard him call.

I went on—this was nothing new; it was always twenty minutes—remembering, as I had done now for the past two years whenever I approached a strange house, that I had lost a friend this way. It was in Virginia, after Second Bull Run, the hot first day of September, '62. The two of us, separated from our command in the retreat, walked up to a roadside cabin to ask the way, and someone fired at us from behind a shuttered window. I ran out of range before the man (or woman; I never knew) could reload, and by the time I got up courage enough to come back, half an hour later, no one was there except my friend, lying in the yard in his gaudy zouave uniform with his knees drawn up and both hands clapped tight against his belt buckle. He looked pinch-faced and very dead, and it seemed indeed a useless way to die.

That was while I was still just Private Lundy, within a month of the day I enlisted back home in Cashtown; that was my baptism of fire, as they like to call it. After that came Antietam and Fredericksburg, where I won my stripes. The war moved fast in those days and while I was in Washington recovering from my Chancellorsville wound I received my commission and orders to report directly to the War Department after a twenty-day convalescent leave. I enjoyed the visit home, limping on a cane and having people admire my new shoulder straps and fire-gilt buttons. "Adam, you're looking fit," they said, pretending not to notice the ruined knee. 'Fit' was their notion of a soldier word, though in fact the only way any soldier ever used it was as the past tense of fight.

When I reported back to the capital I was assigned to the West, arriving during the siege of Vicksburg and serving as liaison officer on one of the gunboats. Thus I missed the fighting at Gettysburg, up near home. It was not unpleasant duty. I had a bed to sleep in, with sheets, and three real meals every twenty-four hours, plus coffee in the galley whenever I wanted it. We shot at them, they shot at us: I could tell myself I was helping to win the war. Independence Day the city fell, and in early August I was ordered to report for duty with Colonel Nathan Frisbie aboard the gunboat *Starlight*. Up till then it had all been more or less average, including the wound; there were thousands like me. But now it changed, and I knew it from the first time I saw him.

He looked at me hard with his one gray eye before returning the salute. "Glad to have you aboard," he said at last. A Negro corporal was braced in a position of exaggerated attention beside a stand of colors at the rear of the cabin. "Orderly," the colonel said. The corporal rolled his eyes. "Show the lieutenant his quarters."

Next morning at six o'clock the corporal rapped at the door of my cabin, then entered and gave me the colonel's compliments, along with instructions to report to the orderly room for a tour of inspection before breakfast. I'd been asleep; I dressed in a hurry, flustered at being late on my first day of duty. Colonel Frisbie was checking the morning report when I came in. He glanced up and said quietly, "Get your saber, Mr Lundy." I returned to my cabin, took the saber out of its wrappings, and buckled it on. I hadnt worn it since the convalescent leave, and in fact hadnt thought I'd ever wear it again.

The troops were on the after deck, each man standing beside his pallet; the colonel and I followed the first sergeant down the aisle. From time to time Colonel Frisbie would pause and lift an article from the display of equipment on one of the pads, then look sharply at the owner before passing on. "Take his name, Sergeant." Their dark faces were empty of everything, but I saw that each man trembled slightly while the colonel stood before him.

After breakfast Colonel Frisbie called me into the orderly room for a conference. This was the first of many. He sat at his desk, forearms flat along its top, the patch over his eye dead black like a target center, his lips hidden beneath the blousy, slightly grizzled mustache. There was hardly any motion in his face as he spoke.

When Vicksburg fell, the colonel said, Mr Lincoln announced that the Mississippi "flowed unvexed to the sea." But, like so many political announcements, this was not strictly true; there was still considerable vexation in the form of sniping from the levee, raids by bodies of regular and irregular cavalry—bushwhackers, the colonel called them—and random incidents involving plunder and disrespect to the flag. So while Sherman sidestepped his way to Atlanta, commanders of districts flanking the river were instructed to end all such troubles. On the theory that partisan troops could not function without the support of the people who lived year-round in the theater, the commanders adopted a policy of holding the civilian population responsible.

"They started this thing, Mr Lundy," the colonel said. "They began it, sir, and while they had the upper hand they thought it was mighty fine. Remember the plumes and roses in those days? Well, *we're* top dog now, East and West, and we'll give them what they blustered for. Indeed. We'll give them war enough to last the time of man."

He brooded, his face in shadow, his hands resting within the circle of yellow lamplight on his desk. I wondered if this silence, which seemed long, was a sign that the conference was over. But just as I was about to excuse myself, the colonel spoke again. He cleared his throat. "Lieutenant, does that knee bother you?"

"Not often, sir. Just when—"

"Never you mind," Colonel Frisbie said, and moving one hand suddenly to the lamp he turned the wick up full and tilted the shade so that the light was thrown directly on his face. His expression was strained, the patch neat and exact. "Theyll pay for that knee, lieutenant. And they will pay for this!" He lifted the patch onto his forehead. The empty socket pulsed as red and raw as when the wound was new.

During the year that followed, the colonel spoke to me often of these and other things. Every morning there was a meeting in the orderly room after breakfast—'conferences' he called them, but he did the talking. I understood how he felt about the eye, the desire to make someone pay for its loss; I had felt it myself about the ruined knee and the death of my friend in Virginia, until I reminded myself, in the case of the knee, that the bullets flew both ways, and in the case of my friend that it was primarily a question of whose home was being invaded. I had more or less put it behind me, this thought of repayment; but with Colonel Frisbie it was different, and for many reasons. He was a New Englander, a lawyer in civilian life, an original abolitionist. He had been active in the underground railroad during the '50s, and when war came he entered the army as a captain under Frémont in Saint Louis. These were things he told me from time to time, but there were things he did not tell, things I found out later.

He had been with Sherman at Shiloh, a major by then, adjutant in an Indiana regiment which broke badly under the Sunday dawn attack. He was near the bluff above Pittsburg Landing, using the flat of his saber on stragglers, when a stray minié came his way with a spent whine and took out his left eye: whereupon he went under the bluff, tore off his shoulder straps, and lay down among the skulkers. There were ten thousand others down there, including officers, and only a few of them wounded; he had better provocation than most. Yet he could not accept it in the way those others apparently could. When the battle was over he bandaged his eye with a strip from his shirt, rejoined his regiment, and later was commended in reports. There were men in his outfit, however, including some of his own clerks, who had also been under the bluff, and he saw them looking at him as if to say, "If you wont tell on me, I wont on you." Soon afterwards he was assigned to courts martial duty with the Adjutant General's Department. When the army adopted its reprisal policy in the lower Mississippi Valley, he was given another promotion and a gunboat with special troops aboard to enforce it.

Patrolling the river from Vicksburg north to Memphis, two hundred and fifty air-line miles and almost twice that far by water, One-Eye Frisbie and the *Starlight* became well known throughout the delta country. Where partisan resistance had once been strongest, soon there was little activity of any kind. It became a bleak region, populated only by women and children and old men and house servants too feeble to join the others gone as 'contraband' with the Union armies. The fields lay fallow, last year's cotton drooping on dead brown stalks. Even the birds went hungry, what few remained. The land was desolated as if by plague.

The only protest now was an occasional shot from the levee, which was followed by instant reprisal in accordance with the Army policy. Colonel Frisbie would tie up at the nearest river town, sending word for evacuation within twenty minutes, and then would give the *Starlight* gunners half an hour's brisk drill, throwing explosive shells over the levee and into the empty buildings and streets where chickens and dogs fluttered and slunk and squawked and howled. Or he would tie up at the point where the sniping occurred, lead the troops ashore, and march them overland sometimes as far as a dozen miles to burn an isolated plantation house.

I was with him from the beginning and I remember him mainly as straddled in silhouette before the lick and soar of flames. Dispossessed, the family huddled somewhere in the background. At first they had been arrogant, threatening reprisal by Forrest or Jameson or Van Dorn. "You had better burn the trees as well," one woman told us. "When we first came there was nothing but woods and we built our homes. We'll build them again." But when Atlanta was besieged their defiance faltered, and when Sherman had taken the city and was preparing for the march that would "make Georgia howl," they knew they were beaten and their armies would never return. There had been a time when they sent their plantation bells and even their brass doorknobs to be melted for cannon; but not any more. Now the war had left them. They were faced with the aftermath before the finish.

Colonel Frisbie looked upon all this as indemnity collectible for the loss of his eye and his courage at Shiloh. Saber and sash and gray eye glinting firelight, he would watch a house burn with a smile that was more like a grimace, lip lifted to expose the white teeth clamping the cigar. That was the way I remembered him now as I continued to walk up the driveway toward the house. Around one of its corners I saw that the outbuildings had already burned, and I wondered if it had been done by accident—a not uncommon plantation mishap—or by one of our armies passing through at the time of the Vicksburg campaign. Then, nearing the portico, I saw that the door was ajar. Beyond it I could see into a high dim hall where a staircase rose in a slow curve. I stood in the doorway, listening, then rapped.

The rapping was abrupt and loud against the silence. Then there was only vacancy, somehow even more empty than before.

"Hello!" I cried, my voice as reverberant as if I had spoken from the bottom of a well. "Hello in there!"

I had a moment of sharp fear, a sudden vision of someone crouched at the top of the staircase, sighting down a rifle barrel at me with a hot, unwinking eye. But when I bent forward and peered, there was no one, nothing. I went in.

Through a doorway on the right I saw a tall black man standing beside an armchair. He wore a rusty claw-hammer coat with buttons of tarnished brass, and on his head there was what appeared to be a pair of enormous white horns. Looking closer I saw that the Negro had bound a dinner napkin about his jaws, one of which was badly swollen, and had tied it at the crown of his head so that the corners stood up stiffly from the knot like the ears on a rabbit. The armchair was wide and deep; it faced the cold fireplace, its high, fan-shaped back turned toward the door.

I said, "Didnt you hear me calling?" The Negro just

stood there, saying nothing. It occurred to me then that he might be deaf; he had that peculiar, vacant look on his face. I came forward. "I said didnt . . ."

But as I approached him, obliquing to avoid the chair, I saw something else.

There was a hand on the chair arm. Pale against the leather and mottled with dark brown liver spots, it resembled the hand of a mummy, the nails long and narrow, almond-shaped. Crossing to the hearth I looked down at the man in the chair, and the man looked up at me. He was old—though old was hardly word enough to express it; he was ancient—with sunken cheeks and a mass of white hair like a mane, obviously a tall man and probably a big one, once, but thin now to the point of emaciation, as if he had been reduced to skin and skeleton and only the most essential organs, heart and lungs and maybe bowels, though not very much of either—'Except heart; there's plenty of that,' I thought, looking into the cold green eyes. His chin, resting upon a high stock, trembled as he spoke.

"Have you brum to run my howl?" he said.

I stared at him. "How's that?" I asked. But the old man did not answer.

"He hyar you, captain," the Negro said. His enormous horns bobbed with the motion of his jaw. "He hyar you well enough, but something happen to him lately he caint talk right."

This was Isaac Jameson, who was born in a wilderness shack beside the Trace while his father, a South Carolina merchant, was removing his family and his business to the Natchez District as part of a caravan which he and other Loyalists had organized to escape the Revolution on the seaboard. Thus in later years, like so many of the leaders of his time, Isaac was able to say in truth that he was a log cabin boy. But it was misleading, for his father, who had prospered under the Crown back east, became even wealthier in the west, and Isaac grew up in a fine big house on the bluff overlooking the river. From the gallery he could watch Spanish sentries patrolling the wharf where steamboats, up from New Orleans, put in with goods for the Jameson warehouse. He was grown, twenty years old and four inches over six feet tall, when John Adams sent troops to take over for the United States and created the Mississippi Territory. The Republic, which his father had come seven hundred miles to escape, had dogged his heels.

Isaac was sixth among eight sons, and he was unlike the others. It was not only that he stood half a head taller; there was some intrinsic difference. They were reliable men, even the two younger ones who followed the removal. But Isaac would not stand at a desk totting figures or checking bills of lading. He was off to cockfights or horseraces, and he spent more evenings in the Under-the-Hill section than he did in Natchez proper. His father, remembering the shack by the Trace, the panthers screaming in the outward darkness while his wife was in labor, believed that his son—wilderness born, conceived in a time of revolution—had received in his blood, along with whatever it was that had given him the extra height and the unaccountable width of his shoulders, some goading spark of rebellion, some fierce, hot distillate of the jungle itself.

Then one day he was gone. He did not say where he was going, or even that he was leaving; he just went. Then ten years later he turned up again, with a bad leg wound from the Battle of New Orleans. He was a year mending. Then he spent another year trying to make up for lost time. But it did not go right. There were still the cockfights and the grog shops and the women under the hill, but the old life had palled on him. He was thirty-nine, a bachelor, well into middle age, and apparently it had all come to nothing.

Then he found what he had been seeking from the start, though he did not know he was looking for it until some time after he found it. Just before his fortieth birthday—in the spring of 1818; Mississippi had entered the Union in December—he rode into the northern wilderness with two trappers who had come to town on their annual spree. This time he was gone a little over two years. Shortly after the treaty of Doaks Stand opened five and a half million acres of Choctaw land across the middle of the state, he reappeared at his father's house. He was in buckskins, his hair shoulder length.

Next day he was gone for good, with ten of his father's Negroes and five thousand dollars in gold in his saddle-bags. He had come back to claim his legacy, to take this now instead of his share in the Jameson estate when the old man died. The brothers were willing, since it would mean a larger share for them when the time came. The father considered it a down-right bargain; he would have given twice that amount for Isaac's guarantee to stay away from Natchez with his escapades and his damage to the name. He said, "If you want to play prodigal it's all right with me. But mind you: when youre swilling with swine and chomping the husks, dont cut your eyes around in my direction. There wont be any lamp in the window, or fatted calf either. This is all."

It was all Isaac wanted, apparently. Between sunup and nightfall of the following day—a Sunday, early in June—they rolled forty miles along the road connecting hamlets north of Natchez. Sundown of the third day they made camp on the near bank of the Yazoo, gazing

down off the Walnut Hills, and Wednesday they entered
the delta, a flat land baked gray by the sun wherever it
exposed itself, which was rare, from under the inter-
twined branches of sycamores and water oaks and cot-
tonwoods and elms. Grass grew so thick that even the
broad tires of the Conestoga left no mark of passage.
Slow, circuitous creeks, covered with dusty scum and
steaming in the heat, drained east and south, away from
the river, each doubling back on itself in convulsive
loops and coils like a snake fighting lice. For four days
then, while the Negroes clutched desperately at seats
and stanchions in a din of creaking wood and clattering
metal (they had been warehouse hands, townspeople,
and ones the brothers could easiest spare at that) the
wagon lurched through thickets of scrub oak and
stunted willow and over fallen trunks and rotted
stumps. It had a pitching roll, like that of a ship riding a
heavy swell, which actually did cause most of the Negroes to become seasick four hundred miles from salt
water.

They followed no trail, for there was no trail to follow. There was only Isaac, who rode a claybank mare as
far out front as visibility allowed, sometimes half a mile,
sometimes ten feet, and even in the latter case they
sometimes followed not the sight of him but the sound
of snapping limbs and Isaac's cursing. Often they had to
dismount with axes and chop through. Just before noon
of the eighth day, Sunday again, they struck the southern end of a lake, veered right, then left, and continued
northward along its eastern shore. Two hours later Isaac
reined in the mare, and when the wagon drew abreast
he signaled for a halt. A wind had risen, ruffling the
lake; through the screen of cypresses the waves were
bright like little hatchets in the sunlight. "All right," he
said. "You can get the gear unloaded. We are home."

That was the beginning. During the next ten years he was joined by others drawn from the south and east to new land available at ninety cents an acre with few questions asked. The eighteen hundred acres of Isaac's original claim were increased to thirty-two hundred in 1826 when his neighbors north and south went broke in the crash. Two years later, though he had named his ten-square-mile plantation Solitaire in confirmation of his bachelor intentions, he got married. It happened almost accidentally. She was the youngest of four daughters; the other three were already married, and she herself was more or less engaged at the time to the blacksmith's assistant, two doors down the street. Her father kept a tavern, and from time to time she took her turn at the tap. Isaac found her tending bar one warm spring evening when he rode down for a drink. He had seen her before, of course, though he had not really noticed. Now he did. He particularly admired her arms, which were bared to the elbows, and her thick yellow hair, worn shoulder length. That night he had trouble getting to sleep. At last he dropped off, however. He did not dream, but when he woke he thought immediately of her. Whats this? he asked himself. He returned to the Inn that evening, and the next. By then he had decided. He spoke to the father first. "I'm willing if Katy is," the innkeeper said.

The wedding was held at the Tavern and the blacksmith's young assistant was there, bulging his biceps, drunk for the first time in his life. He got into three fights that day, though not with Isaac.

2

That ended the first phase of his life, the fifty years spent running hard after trouble in any form, first among men—river bullies at Natchez-under-the-Hill, painted Creeks at Burnt Corn, British regulars at New Orleans; he had tried them all—and then against the cat- and snake-infested jungles of the South. Isaac, however, was not aware that it had ended until two years later, after Dancing Rabbit opened the remaining northern section of the state to settlers, when his neighbors, small farmers and planters alike, were selling their claims for whatever they could get, packing their carts and Conestogas, and heading north into the rich new land that lay between the lake and the Tennessee line. It was then, after they had gone and he had stayed, that Isaac knew his wilderness thirst had been slaked.

What bound him finally and forever to this earth, however—and he knew it—was the birth of his son in August, 1833, the year the stars fell. Mrs Jameson named him Clive, not for any particular reason; she just liked the name. In the ten following years she bore six more children. They were all girls and were all either born dead or died within a week. They lay in a cedar grove, beneath a row of crosses. She had become a pleasant-faced, bustling woman, rather full-bodied, expending her energy on a determination to keep the Jameson house the finest on the lake.

This took some doing: for, though nowhere near the extent it would reach ten years later in the expansive early '50s, there was already plenty of competition. Cotton was coming into its own, and the lake country was a district of big plantations, thousand- and two- and three-thousand-acre places which the owners ruled like barons. When the small farmers, settlers who had followed Isaac into the region after the Doaks Stand treaty opened the land, moved away to the north after Dancing Rabbit—usually with no more than they had had when they arrived, a wagon and a team of mules or

oxen, a rifle and a couple of sticks of furniture, a hound
or two and a crate of chickens or shoats, a wife and a
stair-stepped parcel of children in linsey-woolsey, and
perhaps a widowed mother or mother-in-law—their
claims were gobbled up by those who stayed, as well as
by others who moved in on their heels. These last, the
second wave of comers, were essentially businessmen.
They had no gift (or, for that matter, desire) for ringing
trees and rooting stumps; their gift was rather for organization. They could juggle figures and balance books
and put the profits where they earned more profits. Eli
Whitney made them rich and now they began to build
fine houses to show it, calling them Westoak Hall and
Waverly and Briartree, proud-sounding names in imitation of those in the tide-water counties of Virginia,
though in fact the Virginians were few among them.
They were mostly Kentuckians and North Carolinians,
arrived by way of East Mississippi or the river, and for
the most part they were not younger sons of established
families, sent forth with the parental blessing and gold
in their saddlebags. Many of them did not know their
grandparents' names, and some of them had never
known their fathers.

Isaac's original L-shaped structure, which he and
the ten slaves had put up in 1820 soon after their arrival, had grown now to a two-story mansion with a
brick portico and concrete pillars; the roof had been
raised so that now all the bedrooms were upstairs. It
was still called Solitaire though the name no longer fit.
Isaac himself had grown handsomer with age. He was
still a big man, six feet four, but he looked slimmer and,
somehow, even fitter and more hale. Gray hair became
him. Dressed habitually in broadcloth and starched
linen, he had a stiffness, a formality that resembled an
outward show of self-satisfaction and pride. In 1848,

when he was seventy, people seeing him on the street in Ithaca, with his straight-backed manner of walking and his careful way of planting his feet, would point him out to visitors. "That's Ike Jameson," they would say. "He was the first man into these parts. Fine-looking, aint he. How old would you take him to be?" The visitor would guess at fifty, fifty-five, and his host would laugh. "Seventy. Seventy, by God. Youd never think it, would you? to look at him."

In September of that year he sent his son, who had reached fifteen the month before, to the Virginia Military Institute. This was at the boy's insistence, and Isaac was willing: not because he wanted him to become a soldier (he wanted no such thing; he had known too many soldiers in his time) but because in preparation for the life of a planter it did not much matter what form the schooling took. In fact a military school was probably best, since the boy would be less likely to become seriously involved with books. A young man's true education began when he was through with school and had come back home to learn the running of the plantation, the particular temper and whims of cotton as well as the temper and whims of the people who worked it, meaning Negroes. Besides, the Mexican War was recently over. Young men throughout the South were admiring General Winfield Scott and old Rough-and-Ready Taylor, Captain Bragg the artilleryman who "gave them a little more grape," and Colonel Davis from down near Natchez who formed his regiment, the Mississippi Rifles, in a V at Buena Vista and won the battle with a single charge.

Early in June, nine months later, when Isaac went to Bristol to meet him at the station, Clive was in uniform, the buttons bright against black facings on the slate-gray cloth. All down the platform, people were looking at him. Isaac was impressed.

"I declare, boy, you look almost grown to me."

"Hello, papa," he said, and extended his hand. Always before that they had kissed.

Three Junes later, when he came home from graduation, tall, slim, handsome, blond, nineteen, he was the catch of the lake. It was not only his looks; he could be amusing, too, as for instance when he gave an imitation of his mathematics instructor, T. J. Jackson, who wound up every lecture covered with chalkdust and perspiration and who sometimes became so interested in solving algebra and trigonometry problems that he forgot the students were present and just stood there reasoning with himself and Euclid. Clive had much success with this; "Give us Professor Jackson," they would beg him in houses along the lake. Soon, however, his social horizon widened. He was one of the real catches of the delta. Isaac and Mrs Jameson were impressed, and so were the various girls; but the ones who were most impressed were the girls' mothers. They preened their daughters, set their caps, and laid their snares. At dances and outings he moved among them, attentive, grave, pleasant, quite conscious of the advantages of his position.

Isaac was amused, but he was also rather awed. His own youth had been so different. Past seventy, nearing eighty, he could look back on a life divided neatly into two unequal compartments, the first containing fifty years of wildness and the second containing twenty-odd—nearly thirty—years of domesticity, with marriage like an airtight door between them. Now, though he did not know it and could have done nothing about it anyhow, he was moving toward another door which led to a third compartment, less roomy than ei-

ther of the other two, with a closer atmosphere, even
stifling in the end, and more different from both of the
previous two than those two had been different from
each other. In a sense beyond longevity he led three
lives in one.

Since 1850, the year of the Compromise, planters in
the lake region had been talking disunion. As a topic for
discussion it had crowded out the weather and even the
cotton market. Seated on their verandas or in their par-
lors, clutching juleps in their fists, they blustered. They
had built their fine big neo-Tidewater houses, display-
ing them to their neighbors and whoever passed along
the lakeside road, each as a sort of patent of nobility, a
claim to traditions and ancestry which they for the most
part lacked. Insecurity had bred a semblance of security,
until now no one questioned their right to anything at
all. When Lincoln was nominated in 1860 they took it as
a pointed insult. Not that they believed he would be
elected; no; "Never in all this world," they said. "Those
abolitionist scoundrels just want to flaunt this ape in
our faces for the purpose of watching our reaction. Yes.
Well, we'll show them something in the way of action
they havent bargained for, if they dont watch out. Let
them be warned," they added solemnly.

They admired the spirit and emulated the manner
of the Texas senator, an ex-South Carolinian with a reputation as a duelist, who said to his Northern fellow-
senators, smiling as he said it though not in friendliness
at all: "The difficulty between you and us, gentlemen, is
that you will not send the right sort of people here. Why
will you not send either Christians or gentlemen?"

"Wigfall knows how to treat them," the planters
said. "A few more like him and Preston Brooks and
we'd have this hooraw hushed."

But Isaac, who had fought under Andrew Jackson

at New Orleans and followed his politics ever since, believed in the Union in much the same way as Jackson
had believed in it. He thought sectional differences
could be solved better within the Union than outside it.
At first he would say so, with the others watching him
hot-eyed over the frosted rim of goblets. Later he saw
that it was no use. Like much of the rest of the nation,
they were determined to have violence as the answer to
some deep-seated need, as actual as thirst.

Clive took little or no part in these discussions
which went on all around him. He had come home from
the Institute with a soldier's training, but now he was
busy learning the life of a planter; the slate-gray uniforms and the tactics texts had been folded away in a
trunk with the unblooded sword. He was closer to his
mother than he was to Isaac. He was quiet, indeed
somewhat vague in his manner, with gentle eyes; his
way now was very little different, in fact, from the way
in which he had moved among the Bristol matrons and
fanned their hopes with his almost casual attentiveness.
He loved horses and spent much of his time in the sta-
bles. Behind the softness of his eyes and voice there was
something wild that matched the wildness of horses,
and this was where he most resembled his father.

Then Lincoln was elected—the planters had said it
would never happen; "Never in all this world," they
said—and South Carolina seceded, followed within two
weeks by Mississippi and then the others among the
Deep South fire-eater states. That was in January. Mod-
eration was gone now, what little had remained. Clive
even heard from the Institute that the chalkdusty Professor Jackson, a Mexican War veteran himself, had
stood up in chapel and made a speech; "Draw the
sword and throw away the scabbard!" he had cried. It
did not sound at all like him, but anything was believ-

able in these times. Two months later, a month before
Sumter, Clive rode off as captain of a cavalry troop
formed by the lake planters and their sons. With their
wagons, their spare mounts and body servants, they
made a long column; their ornaments flashed in the
sunlight.

Nearly all of them returned within four months,
not as a unit but in straggling twos and threes. It was
the common end of such 'elite' organizations; they had
not expected war to be like that. The excitement lasted
not even as long as the glitter of their collar ornaments.
Once it was gone they thought they might as well come
home. They had seen no fighting anyhow. It was mostly
drill and guard mount, patrolling encampments while
the infantry slept, moving from place to place, then back
again. The glory had departed, and so did they.

When Clive came home, his uniform and saber sash
a bit faded from the weather, Isaac came out to meet
him in the yard, looking somehow more military in
broadcloth than his son looked in uniform. They stood
looking at each other. "How did it go?" Isaac asked
him.

"It went all right, considering. There just wasnt
anything to do."

"You wanted it another way. Was that it?"

"I didnt want it the way it was. We disbanded
piecemeal, man by man. They would come and say they
were leaving. Then theyd leave. Finally there were less
than a dozen of us; so we left too. We made it official."

They stood facing each other in the hot summer
sunlight; First Manassas had been fought two weeks
ago. Clive was smiling. Isaac did not smile. "And what
are you going to do now?" he asked. "Stay here and
farm the place?"

"I might."

"So?"

"I might. . . ."

"So?"

"No, papa. I'll go back. But different."

"So," Isaac said.

He stayed ten days, and then he left again. This time he went alone. Within two years Clive Jameson was one of the sainted names of the Confederacy. It began when he came out of Donelson with Forrest, escaping through icy backwater saddle-skirt deep. Then he distinguished himself at Shiloh, leading a cavalry charge against the Peach Orchard and another at Fallen Timbers after the battle; Beauregard cited him as one of the heroes of that field. By the time of Vicksburg, in the summer of '63, newspapers were beginning to print the story of his life. Southern accounts always mentioned his having been born the year the stars fell; Starborn, one called him, and the others took it up. Poetesses laureate in a hundred backwoods counties submitted verse in which they told how he had streamed down to earth like a meteor to save the South; they made much of the flaming wake. Northern accounts, on the other hand, made much of the fact that his mother had tended bar in her father's taproom.

He never wrote. They did not see him again until late in '63 when he was wounded at Chickamauga, his fifth but his first really serious wound, and was brought home in an ambulance to recover. He was still a young man, just past his thirtieth birthday, but he looked older than his years. It was as if the furnace of war had baked the flesh of his hard, handsome face, which by now was tacked in replica on cabin walls, badly reproduced pen-and-ink sketches clipped from newspapers, and mooned over by girls in attic bedrooms. The softness had gone from his eyes and voice. He did not resemble

himself; he resembled his pictures. Having him at Solitaire was like having a segment of some actual blasted
battlefield at hand. His mother, after an hour with him,
came away shaking her head. "What have they done to
my boy?" she asked.

"He's a hero," Isaac said. He had seen and known
heroes before. "What did you expect?"

Clive mended fast, however, and soon after the first
of the year he rode away. They heard of his raid into
Kentucky that spring—'brilliant' was the word that appeared most frequently in the newspaper accounts; the
columns bristled with it, alongside 'gallant'—and in
June he led his brigade in the attack that crumpled
Grierson's flank at Brice's Crossroads and sent the invaders stumbling back to Memphis. The papers were
full of it, prose and verse.

Mrs Jameson sealed off the upper story of her
house. She and Isaac lived downstairs. She was fifty-six,
an active, bustling woman who got things done. She
still had the yellow hair and even the beautifully
rounded arms, but she was subject to dizzy spells,
which she called the Vapors, and during such an attack
her mind would wander. She would imagine the war
was over and her son was dead. A moment later,
though, she would sigh and say, "I'm glad he's doing
well, but I wish they would let him come home for a
while. I really do."

She never thought of him the way he had been
when he was there with his Chickamauga wound. In
her mind she saw him as he had been when he rode
away that first time, in the spring of '61, with the soft
voice and gentle eyes, or as he was in the daguerreotype
which she kept on the night table beside her bed. It had
been taken when he was a child; he wore button shoes
and ribbed stockings and a jacket of watered silk, and

there was a small-boy sweetness in his face. Sometimes in the night Isaac would wake to find the candle burning at the bedside and Mrs Jameson sitting bolt upright, propped on three pillows, with the picture in her hands. There would be tears in her eyes, and if he spoke to her at such a time she would turn and look at him with the face of a stranger.

On a hot July morning she was waxing the dining room table—a task she had always reserved for herself because it gave her a particular pleasure—when suddenly she paused and a peculiar expression came over her face, the expression of someone about to sneeze. Then she did; she sneezed loudly. "God bless me," she said, automatically, and went on with her work, applying the wax in long, even strokes. Presently she raised one hand to her forehead, palm outward, fingers relaxed. "I feel so dizzy," she said. She looked frightened. Isaac reached her just as she fell. He carried her to a couch in the living room and knelt beside her, patting her wrists. Her breath came in harsh stertorous groans.

"Katy!" Isaac kept saying. "Katy, dont you know me?"

She did not know him; she did not know anything. Foam kept forming on her lips and Isaac wiped it away with his handkerchief. Two Negroes stood in the background. There was nothing they could do. All the doctors were off to war, but that was just as well since there was nothing they could have done either. It was a cerebral hemorrhage and she died within four hours.

Next day they buried her in the cedar grove, at the near end of the row of small, weathered crosses. Isaac was dry-eyed at the burial; he did not seem to understand what had happened. He was bewildered at last by mortality, by a world in which a person could sneeze and say, "God bless me: I feel dizzy," and then be dead. He was eighty-six years old.

3

All but three of the slaves had left by then, gone on their own or as dish-washers and ditch-diggers with the Union armies which had roamed the district at will and without real opposition since early '64. There was Edward, the butler, who was almost seventy, the last of the original ten who had come with Isaac in the Conestoga north from Natchez. He was stone deaf, a tall, straight-backed Negro, mute and inscrutable behind his wall of dignity and deafness. The other two were women; both were old, one lame (she did the cooking, what there was to cook) and the other half-witted. These three lived in one of the cabins that formed a double row, called the Quarters, half a mile behind the house. The other cabins were empty, beginning to dry rot from disuse, and the street between the rows, formerly grassless, polished by generations of bare feet until it was almost as smooth and shiny as a ballroom floor, was beginning to spring up in weeds. When Mrs Jameson died Edward moved into the house with Isaac. Five weeks later the two women joined them because a Federal platoon, out on patrol, burned the quarters.

That was in August. Near sundown the platoon made bivouac in a pasture near the house. The cooks set up their kitchen and sent out a three-man detail for firewood. They were tearing up the floorboards in one of the cabins, the planks making sudden, ripping sounds like musketry, when one of the soldiers happened to glance up and see a tall yellow woman, her face pitted with old smallpox scars, standing in the doorway watching them. She clasped her wrists over her stomach and watched them gravely. It gave him a start, finding her there like that without having heard her approach.

"Yawl bed not be doing that," she said when the soldier looked at her.

The others paused too, now. They stood leaning forward with half-ripped planks in their hands. Their uniforms were dusty, still sweaty from marching all that afternoon. "Why not, aunty?" the first said. His speech was Southern, though obviously from north of Mississippi.

"I'll tell Mars Ike and he'll tell his boy: thats why. And the genril he'll come back and git you, too, what time he hears you messing with his belongings like you doing."

They resumed their work, tearing up the floorboards with a splintering, ripping sound, and the sunlight slanting through the western window was filled with dust-motes. Then one of them said casually, "What general would that be, aunty?"

"Genril Cli Jameson, Mars Ike's boy. You see if I dont."

Again they paused, once more with the ends of half-ripped planks in their hands. But this time it was different. They looked at her, all three together, and something like joy was registered on their faces. "Does this belong to him, that house and all these shanties?"

"Does indeed, and you best quit or I'll tell him. I'm a mind to tell him anyhow, the way yawl acting."

"Well," the first said, still not moving, still bent forward. "Well, well. What do you know."

Then he moved. He finished prizing up the plank he had hold of, took a jackknife from his pocket, one of the big horn-handled ones the suttlers sold in such volume every payday, and began to peel shavings from the edge of the plank. It was cypress, long since cured, and

the shavings came off straight and clean, a rich pink
almost red. The other two watched him for a moment,
puzzled. Then they understood and began to do the
same, taking out their knives and peeling shavings from
other planks. They worked in silence, all three together.
They were from a Tennessee Union regiment—what
their enemies called home-made Yankees. All three had
week-old beards.

"That damned butcher," the third said. He had not
spoken until now. "Aint it funny what luck will sometimes throw your way?"

The woman watched them without understanding,
still with her hands crossed on the bulge of her stomach, while one of the soldiers scraped the shavings into
a small pile in one corner of the room. He laid planks
across it, first the split ones and then whole ones, building a tepee of lumber. When he had finished this he
took a tinder box from the pocket of his blouse, then
bent and struck it so that a shower of sparks fell into the
heart of the little heaped-up pile of cypress shavings. At
first it merely smoked and glowed. Suddenly a flame
leaped up, bright yellow, then orange, then rose-
colored, licking the wall of the cabin.

"Yawl bed not be doing that," the woman said
again, her voice as flat, as inflectionless as at the start.

The soldiers stood watching the fire. When it was
burning nicely they gathered up the remainder of their
ripped-up floorboards and started for the pasture where
by now the cook had begun to beat with a big spoon
against the bottom of a dishpan to hurry them along.
One paused at the foot of the steps, turning with the
bundle of planks on his shoulder. The others stopped
beyond him, looking back and smiling as he spoke.
"Tell him thats for Fort Pillow, aunty. Tell him it's from
the friend of a man who was there."

Fifteen minutes later Isaac and Edward and the lame cook, and presently the half-witted woman too, stood on the back gallery and watched the quarters burn. "I told um not to, plain as I'm standing here talking to you right now," the woman said. There was no wind, not a breath; the flames went straight up with a sucking, roaring sound like the rush of something passing at great speed. Even deaf Edward, though he could not hear it, felt its deep murmuring whoosh against his face. He turned his head this way and that, as if he had recovered his hearing after all those years of silence.

The Federal platoon, the men in collarless fatigue blouses and galluses, many of them smoking pipes while they waited for supper, gathered at the back of the pasture to watch the progress of the fire. They leaned their elbows on the top rail of the fence, and as the dusk came on and the flames spread from cabin to cabin along the double row, flickering brighter and brighter on their faces, they made jokes at one another up and down the line. Soon the cook beat again on the dishpan with the spoon and they lined up with messkits in their hands. The fire burned on. It burned steadily into the night, its red glow reflected against the underside of the pall of smoke hanging over the plantation. From time to time a roof fell in, occasionally two together, and a bright rush of sparks flew upward in a fiery column that stood steadily upright for a long moment, substantial as a glittering pillar of jeweled brass supporting the black overhang of smoke, before it paled and faded and was gone.

Next morning when Isaac came out of the house he found the pasture empty, the soldiers gone, with only an unclosed latrine and a few charred sticks of the cookfire to show they had been there at all. He walked down to where the quarters had been, and there were only the foundation stones and the toppled chimneys, the bricks still hot among the cooling ashes. The cabins had been built during the ten-year bachelor period between his arrival and his marriage—sixteen cabins, two rows of eight, put up during the ten-year span by a five-man building team who snaked the big cypresses out of a slough, split them with axes and crosscut saws for timbers and planks and shingles and even pegs to save the cost of nails. They had been good cabins, snug in winter, cool in summer, built to last; they had seen forty years of living and dying, laughing and weeping, arrival and departure. Now they were gone, burned overnight, casualties of the war.

As he turned at the end of the double row, starting back, a great weariness came over him. He stood there for a moment, arms loose at his sides, then returned to the house. He went up the steps and across the gallery. In the kitchen a strange thing happened to him.

The cook was boiling something on the stove, stirring it with a long-handled spoon, and as he came past he intended to ask her, 'Is breakfast ready?' But that was not what he said. He said, "Is breck us riding?"

"Sir?"

He tried again. "Has bread abiding?"

"Sir?" The cook looked at him. She had turned sideways, still bent forward over the pot, and the spoon dripped a thin white liquid. It was cornmeal mush; she would boil it to a thicker consistency, then cook it into cakes to be served with sorghum. With her crooked leg, bowed back, and lips collapsed about her toothless mouth so that her nose and chin were brought into near conjunction, she resembled a witch. "Sir?" she said.

Isaac made a gesture of impatience and went on toward the front of the house. His arms and legs were trembling; there was a pulsing sensation in his head, immediately behind his eyes, a throbbing produced by pressure. Something is happening to me! he thought. He could think the words clearly: 'Is breakfast ready?' but when he tried to say them they came out wrong. Words came out that were not even in his mind as he spoke. Something has happened to me! he thought.

These were the first signs of motor aphasia, the words coming wrong from his tongue. They were not always wrong; sometimes he could speak with no trouble at all. But sooner or later a word or a phrase, unconnected with what he intended to say, would substitute itself. Then the lame cook or the half-witted woman, who was supposed to be the housemaid but who actually did nothing, would look at him with puzzled eyes. "Sir?" they would say, feeling awkward. They did not know whether it was a mishap or a joke; they did not know whether to worry or to laugh. So Isaac avoided them, preferring the company of Edward, who did not hear him anyhow, whether the words were correct or wrong, accurate or garbled.

Mostly, though, he kept to himself, avoiding any need for speech. His favorite pastime now was to walk eastward beyond the burnt-out quarters and on to where a Choctaw village had been, a pottery center with its clay deposit which he in his turn had used for making bricks. He remembered the Indians from fifty years ago, going north in their filthy blankets, braves and squaws, dispossessed by a race of men who were not only more cunning but who backed their cunning with gunpowder and whiskey. They were gone now, casualties not of war but of progress, obsolete, and had left no sign of their passing except the shards of pottery and arrowheads turned up by plowmen, the Indian mounds scattered at random about the land for arche-

ologists to guess at, and an occasional lift to the cheek-
bones in a Negro face and a cocoa tint to the skin.

Isaac had never been one for abstract thinking; but
now, reft of his vocation by the war, of his wife by
death, and of speech by whatever had gripped his brain
and tongue, he asked himself certain questions. It was
as if, now that he could no longer voice them, the words
came to him with great clarity of mind. Remembering
the Indian days, the exodus, he applied what he remembered to the present, to himself. Was it all for nothing,
the distances, the ambition, and the labor? He and his
kind, the pioneers, the land-grabbing hungry rough-
shod men who had had, like the flatboat river bullies
before them, that curious combination of bravado and
deadly earnestness, loving a fight for the sake of the
fight itself and not the outcome—were they to disap-
pear, having served their purpose, and leave no more
trace than the Choctaws? If so, where was the dignity of
man, to be thrown aside like this, a worn-out tool? He
remembered the land as it was when he first came, a
great endless green expanse of trees, motionless under
the press of summer or tossing and groaning in the
winds of spring and fall. He ringed them, felled them,
dragged them out; he fired the stumps so that the air
was hazed with the blue smoke of their burning, and
then he had made his lakeside dream a reality; the
plowmen came, the cotton sprouted, and he prospered;
until now. The earth, he thought, the earth endures. He
groped for the answer, dealing with such abstract sim-
plicities for the first time since childhood, back before
memory. The earth, he thought, and the earth goes back
to the sun; that was where it began. There is no law, no
reason except the sun, and the sun doesnt care. Its only
concern is its brightness; we feed that brightness like

straws dropped into its flame. Fire! he thought suddenly. It all goes back to fire!

At last he gave up the walks and spent his days in a big armchair in the parlor, keeping the curtains drawn. He had nothing to do with anyone but the deaf butler, with whom speech was not only unnecessary but impossible. Edward brought him food on a tray, such as it was—mostly the cakes of boiled-down gruel, with sorghum and an occasional piece of sidemeat—but Isaac scarcely touched it. He lost weight; the flesh hung loose on his big frame; his temples were concave, his eyes far back in their sockets. Sometimes, alone in the darkened parlor, he tried to form words aloud, listening to what came out when he spoke. But it was worse than ever. Often, now, the sounds were not even words. I'm talking in the tongues, he thought, remembering the revivals and sanctifyings he had attended around Natchez as a young man, a scoffer on the lookout for excitement. He had seen and heard whole creekbanks full of people writhing and speaking gibberish—'the tongues' they called it; they claimed to understand each other in such fits. God had touched them, they said.

Maybe God had touched him too, he thought. He had never been religious, never having felt the need for it—not even now, when a general revival was spreading through the armies and the civilian population of the South—yet he knew nothing of aphasia, either by name or contact, and it seemed to him there must be some reason why he had been stricken like the fanatics on the creekbank; there must be some connection. But if it was God it was punishment, since it had not come through faith. He must be under judgment, just as maybe the whole nation was, having to suffer for the double sin of slavery and mistreatment of the land. Presently, however, this passed and he let it go; he stopped consider-

ing it at all, and he stopped trying to talk. He went back
to his previous conviction. No, no, he thought, alone in
the parlor with the curtains drawn. It's the sun and we
go back there, back to fire.

In late October, a time of heat—the long hot summer of '64 had held; dust was everywhere over the
empty fields—he was sitting in the armchair and he
heard footsteps on the driveway. There was a chink of
spurs, then boot-heels coming hard up the front steps.
They crossed the veranda. For a moment there was silence, then a rapping of knuckles against the door jamb.
A voice: "Hello!" Another silence, somehow more preg-
nant than the one before. And then: "Hello in there!"

To Isaac all this seemed so loud that even Edward
must have heard it. But when he turned and looked at
him he saw that the butler was still locked behind his
wall of deafness; he stood beside Isaac's chair, looking
morosely at nothing at ail. He had a toothache and the
cook had put a wad of cotton soaked in camphor inside
his cheek, binding the bulged jaw with a dinner napkin
tied at the crown of his head. It was one of Mrs Jameson's best pieces of linen, big and heavy, and the two
corners of the folded napkin stood up stiffly from the
knot.

While Isaac watched, the Negro turned his face
toward the door, his eyes coming suddenly wide with
surprise. Then Isaac heard the voice again, the crisp
Northern accent: "Didnt you hear me out there?" Footsteps approached and the voice began again, repeating
the question, but was cut off by a surprised intake of
breath. Then Isaac saw him. A Federal officer, complete
with sword and sash and buttons stamped US, stood on
the hearth. They looked at one another.

Isaac saw that the officer was a young man—rather
hard-looking, however, as if the face had been baked in

the same crucible that had hardened and glazed the face of his son Clive—and he thought: It's something the war does to them; North and South, they get this way after a time because nowdays the wars go on too long. Then as they looked at each other, one on the hearth and the other in the chair, Isaac knew why the officer was there. He steadied himself to speak, intending to say, 'Have you come to burn my house?' But it did not come out that way; he spoke again in the tongues.

The lieutenant, whose rank Isaac saw when he bent forward, listened to Edward's explanation of the garbled language, then said carefully: "I have come to give you notice, notification." He paused, cleared his throat, and continued. He spoke carefully, not as if he were choosing his words, but as if from a memorized speech. "In reprisal for sniping, by a party or parties unknown, against the gunboat *Starlight* at sundown yesterday, I inform you now, by order of Colonel Nathan Frisbie, United States Army, that this house has been selected to be burned. You have exactly twenty minutes."

Isaac sat watching the hard young face, the moving lips, the bars on the shoulders. The lips stopped, sternset, but he still watched. "Fire," he said or intended to say. "It all began and ends in fire."

Full in our faces the big low blood-red disk of the sun rested its rim on the levee, like a coin balanced lengthwise on a knife edge. We marched westward through a wilderness of briers and canebrakes, along a road that had been cleared by the planters in their palmy days to haul cotton to the steamboat landing for shipment to New Orleans. The column had rounded the head of the lake and turned toward the river where the gunboat waited. Four miles in our rear, beyond the lake, the reflection of the burning house was a rose-and-violet glow to match the sunset in our front.

I rode beside the colonel at the head and the troops plodded behind in a column of fours. They marched at ease, their boots stirring the dust so that those in the center were hidden from the waist down and those at the tail showed only their heads and shoulders. Their rifle barrels, canted in all directions, caught the ruddy, almost level rays of the sun; the bayonets, fixed, appeared to have been blooded. They kept their heads lowered, their mouths tight shut, breathing through their noses. The only sounds were the more or less steady clink of equipment, the soft clop clop of horses' hoofs, and the shuffle of shoes in the dust. It somehow had an air of unreality in the failing light.

While the upper half of the sun still showed above the dark knife edge of the levee we approached a live-oak spreading its limbs above a grassy space beside the road. Colonel Frisbie drew rein and raised one arm to signal a halt. The troops came to a jumbled stop, like freight cars. Then the sergeant advanced and stood beside the colonel's horse, waiting. He was short and muscular, thick-chested and very black, with so little neck that his head seemed to rest directly on his shoulders. "Ten minutes," the colonel told him.

The sergeant saluted, holding it stiffly until the colonel returned it, then faced about. The troops stood in the dust of the road. He drew himself up, taking a deep breath. "De-tail: ten *shut!*" He glared. "Ground— harms!"

Dismounting, the colonel smiled. "Good man," he said. "That comes of having trained him myself."

"Yes sir," I said.

The platoon fell out, coming apart almost unwillingly, like something coming unglued. Colonel Frisbie often declared that, properly trained and led, Negro troops made "the finest soldiers on the planet, bar none," and when he was given command of the *Starlight* he set out to prove his contention by supplying the proper training and leadership. Now he was satisfied; it was no longer a theory, it was a fact. The corporal-orderly took our horses and we crossed the grass and sat with our backs against the trunk of the live-oak. I was glad to rest my knee.

High in the branches a blue jay shrilled and chattered. The colonel looked up, searching, and finally found him. "Isnt today Friday?"

"Yes sir," I said.

"Thought so. Then here's another case of these people not knowing what theyre talking about. They say you never see a jay on a Friday because thats the day theyre all in hell getting instructions from the devil. And they believe it, too—I dont exaggerate." He nodded. Ever since he had heard the fable he had been spending a good part of every Friday watching for a blue jay. It bothered him for a while that he could not find one. But now he had, and he felt better; he could move on to something else, some other old wives' tale to disprove. "I suppose while we're whipping the rebelliousness out of them we'd do well to take out some of the superstition along with it. Hey?"

"Yes sir," I said.

He went on talking and I went on saying Yes sir every time I heard his voice rise to a question. But I was not listening; I could not have repeated a word he said just then. My mind was back on the other side of the lake, where the reflection of the burning house grew brighter against the darkling sky—remembering, then and now:

When I had finished my recitation—"selected to be

burned. You have exactly twenty minutes"—the old
man looked up at me out of a face that was older than
time. He sank back into the chair. "Far," he said; "It
goes back too far," and gave no other sign that he had
understood or even heard what I said. I left the house,
went back down the driveway to where the troops
crouched in loose circles, preparing to eat the bread and
meat, the midday meal they had brought in their haversacks.

Colonel Frisbie was waiting. "What did they say in
there?" he asked.

"It was an old man. . . ."

"Well?"

"Sir?"

"What did he say?"

"He didnt say anything. He just sat there."

"Oh?" the colonel said, turning to accept a packet
of sandwiches from the orderly. This was officers' food.
"Well. Maybe for once we've found one who admits he
deserves what he's going to get. Or maybe it's not his."
He opened the packet, selected a sandwich, and extended the rest toward me. "Here." I shook my head
but he insisted. "Go on. Take one." I took one—it was
mutton—then sat with it untasted in my hand.

The colonel ate rapidly and efficiently, moving his
jaw with a steady sidewise thrust and taking sips from
his canteen between bites. When he had eaten a second
sandwich he took out his watch, opened the heavy silver case, and laid it face-up on his knee. Soon afterwards he picked it up again; he rose, brushed crumbs
from the breast of his uniform, looked hard at the watch
for a few more seconds, then snapped it shut with a
sharp, decisive click.

"All right, Mr Lundy," he said. "Time's up."

I reentered the house with the sergeant and ten of

the men. From the hall I saw the butler still standing in the parlor beside the fanback chair where the old man sat. At a sign from the sergeant, two of the soldiers took position on opposite sides of the chair, then lifted the old man, chair and all, and carried him through the hall, out of the door and across the porch, and set him down at the foot of the lawn, near the road and facing the front of the house. The butler walked alongside, his pink-palmed hands fluttering in time with the tails of his claw-hammer coat, making gestures of caution. "Keerful, yawl," he kept saying in the cracked, off-key voice of the deaf. "Be keerful, now." The napkin-end rabbit ears had broken. One fell sideways, along his jaw, and the other down over his face. He slapped at it from time to time to get it out of his eyes as he stood watching the soldiers set the chair down.

What followed was familiar enough; we had done this at many points along the river between Vicksburg and Memphis, the Walnut Hills and the Lower Chickasaw Bluff, better than two dozen times in the course of a year. The soldiers went from room to room, ripping curtains from the windows and splintering furniture and bed-slats for kindling. When the sergeant reported the preparations complete, I made a tour of inspection, upstairs and down—the upstairs had been closed off for some time now; dust was everywhere, except in one room which apparently was used by one of the servants. At his shouted command, soldiers in half a dozen rooms struck matches simultaneously. (A match was still a rarity but we received a special issue for our work, big sulphur ones that sputtered at first with a great deal of smoke and stench till they burned past the chemical tip.) Then one by one they returned and reported to the sergeant. The sergeant in turn reported to me, and I gave the order to retire. It was like combat,

and all quite military; Colonel Frisbie had worked out
the procedure in a company order a year ago, with sub-
paragraphs under paragraphs and a time-schedule running down the margin.

From the lawn, where we turned to watch, the
house appeared as peaceful, as undisturbed as it had
been before we entered. But soon, one after another,
wisps of smoke began to laze out, and presently a lick
of flame darted and curled from one of the downstairs
windows. As I stood watching the flames begin to catch,
I let my eye wander over the front of the house and I
saw at an upper window the head and shoulders of a
Negro woman. I could see her plainly, even the smallpox scars on her face. She did not seem excited. In fact
she seemed quite calm, even decorous, sitting there
looking out over the lawn where the soldiers by now
were beginning to shout and point: "Look yonder! Look
up yonder!"

I ran toward the house. The smoke and flames were
mostly from the draperies and splintered furniture, I
saw as I entered the hall again, but the smoke was thick
enough to send me into a fit of coughing and I saw the
staircase through a haze of tears. Climbing at a stumbling run I reached the upper hall. The smoke was less
dense here; I managed to choose the door to the proper
bedroom. It was not locked, as I had feared it might be.
I was about to kick it in, but then I tried the knob and it
came open.

The woman sat in a rocking chair beside the window. She had hidden behind some clothes in a closet
while we searched and set fire to the house; then she
had taken her seat by the window, and from time to
time—the gesture was almost coy, coquettish—she
raised one hand to wave at all the soldiers on the lawn.
"Look yonder! Look up yonder!" they still shouted,

pointing, and she waved back, flirtatious. When I stumbled into the room, half blinded by smoke, she turned and looked at me without surprise; I even had the impression that she had been waiting for me to join her.

"Shame," she said solemnly. She wagged a finger at me. "Shame on you, captain, for trying to burn Mars Ike's fine house. I seen you."

The tears cleared and I found myself looking into the woman's eyes. They were dark brown, almost black, the yellowed whites flicked with little points of red, and completely mad. Trapped in a burning house with a raving lunatic: it was something out of a nightmare. I was wondering how to get her to leave, whether to use force or try to persuade her, when she solved everything by saying in a hoarse whisper, as if in fear of being overheard: "Sh. Less us git out of here, fo they burns it." I nodded, afraid to speak because whatever I said might cause her to change her mind. I even bent forward, adopting her air of conspiracy. "Wait," she said. "I'll git my things."

While the flames crackled in an adjoining room, really catching now, she got what she called her 'things' —a big, brass-hinged family Bible and a cracked porcelain chamberpot with a design of overlapping rose leaves about its rim—and we went downstairs together through the smoke, which was considerably thicker now. "Look to me like they done already started to burn it," she said. As we came out onto the lawn the soldiers gave a cheer.

But I did not feel heroic. For one thing, there had been small risk involved; and for another, even that small risk had frightened me badly. The house continued to smoulder and smoke, though little tongues of flame licked murmurous at the sills. This went on for what seemed a very long time, myself thinking as I

watched: Go on, burn! Get it over; burn! And then, as if
in answer, a great billow of flame rushed from a downstairs window, then another from another and another,
rushing, soaring, crackling like laughter, until the whole
front of the house was swathed in flames. It did not
murmur now. It roared.

Those nearest the house, myself among them, gave
back from the press of heat. It came in a rolling wave;
our ears were filled with the roaring until we got far
enough back to hear a commotion in progress at the
opposite end of the lawn, near the road. Turning, we
saw what had happened.

The old man in the chair was making some sort of
disturbance, jerking his arms and legs and wagging his
head. He had been quiet up to this time, but now he
appeared to be making a violent speech. The soldiers
had crowded around, nudging each other and craning
over one another's shoulders for a better view. Then I
got there and I saw what it was. He was having a
stroke, perhaps a heart attack. The butler, still wearing
the absurd napkin bandage about his jaws, stood on one
side of the chair; he bent over the old man, his hands
out toward him. On the other side were two women.
One was lame and witchlike except that now her eyes
were round with fright, the way no witch's ever where;
I had not seen her before. The other was the mad
woman I had brought out of the burning house. She still
clutched the brass-hinged Bible under one arm, and
with the other she had drawn back the chamberpot,
holding it by the wire handle and threatening the soldier onlookers with it. It was heavy and substantial
looking, despite the crack down its curved flank—a formidable weapon. Brandishing it, she shouted at the
soldiers.

"Shame!" she cried, not at all in the playful tone

she had used when she said the word to me in the
house a few minutes before. She was really angry now.
Her smallpox-pitted face was distorted by rage, and her
eyes were wilder than ever. "Whynt you bluebelly hel-
lions let him be? Wicked! Calling yourself soldiers.
Burners is all you is. Aint you hurt him enough aready?
Shame on you!"

By the time I got there, however, the old man was
past being hurt by anyone. The frenzy was finished,
whether it came from the heart or the brain. He
slumped in the chair, his legs thrust forward, knees stiff,
and his arms dropped limp at his flanks, inside the
chair arms. The only sign of life was the harsh breathing
and the wide, staring eyes; he was going. Soon the
breathing stopped, too, and I saw in the dead eyes a
stereoscopic reflection of the burning house repeated in
double miniature. Behind me the flames soared higher,
roaring, crackling. The lame woman dropped to her
knees and began to wail.

These were things I knew would stay with me always, the sound of that scream, the twin reflection in
those eyes. They were with me now as Colonel Frisbie
stood over me, repeating my name: "Lundy. Mr
Lundy!" I looked up, like a man brought suddenly out
of sleep, and saw him standing straddle-legged in high
dusty boots."

"Sir?"

"Come on, Lieutenant. Time to go." He turned and
then looked back. "Whats the matter with you?"

"Yes, sir," I said, not having heard the words themselves, only the questioning tone.

He turned back, and now for the first time in all the
months I had known him, the pretense was gone; he
was a man alone. "Whats the matter?" he said. "Dont
you like me?"

It was out, and as soon as he had said it I could see that he had surprised himself even more than he had surprised me. He wished he could call the question back. But he stood there, still naked to the elements.

"Yes sir," I said. "I have come to feel very close to you through these past fourteen months."

I got up and walked to where the orderly held our horses. Colonel Frisbie came on behind me; for a moment I had almost liked him; God knows he had his problems; but now he was himself again. The troops had already fallen into column on the road. We marched, and the sun was completely gone. Behind us the glow of burning had spread along the eastern sky. As we marched westward through a blue dusk the glow receded, drawing it upon itself. The colonel lit another cigar; its smoke had a strong, tarry smell as its ruby tip shone and paled, on and off and on and off, like a signal lamp. When he turned in the saddle, looking back, leather creaked above the muffled clopping of hoofs in the cooling dust.

"Looks lower," he said. He smoked, still looking back. The cigar glowed. I knew he was watching me, thinking about my answer to his question; he hadnt quite understood it yet. Then he turned to the front again. "Catch quick, burn slow. Thats the way those old ones always go."

I did not answer. I did not look back.

As we went up the levee, having crossed the swampy, canebrake region that lay between the river and the lake—a wilderness belonging less to men than to bears and deer, alligators and moccasins, weird-screaming birds and insects that ticked like clocks in the brush—the colonel drew rein and turned his horse aside for the troops to pass. I took position alongside him on the crest, facing east toward where the reflection had shrunk to a low dome of red. Then suddenly, as we looked across the wilderness and the lake, the house collapsed and loosed a fountain of sparks, a tall column of fire that stood upright for a long minute, solid as a pillar outlined clearly against the backdrop of the night. It rose and held and faded, and the glow was less than before, no more than a gleam.

"Roof fell in," the colonel said. "Thats all, hey?"

I did not answer. I was seeing in my mind the dead face, the eyes with their twin reflection; I was hearing the lame woman scream; I was trying to remember something out of the Book of Job: *Yet man is born unto trouble, as the sparks fly upward.* And: *Man that is born of woman is of few days, and full of trouble. He cometh forth like a flower, and is cut down: he fleeth also as a shadow, and continueth not.* I was still trying to remember the words, but could not, when the last of the troops filed past. The words I remembered were those of the mad woman on the lawn. "Calling yourself soldiers," she said. "Burners is all you is." I twitched the reins, following Colonel Frisbie down the western slope of the levee, over the gang-plank and onto the gunboat again.

Homecoming

An Excerpt from *Ourselves to Know*

JOHN O'HARA

A few weeks after the Fourth of July the noon train brought home two men who had been in the great battle at Gettysburg. Although they wore uniforms they did not seem to be soldiers; they were more like men seen riding home in a wagon after an accident at the colliery. Their beards were untrimmed, their jackets spotted and half buttoned, and one of them could not put on his cap because his head was wrapped in bandage. The other had lost a foot and his pant-leg was folded over and pinned. He could not manage his crutch coming down the steps of the coach and called out: "Will some son of a bitch give me a hand?" But before anyone could reach him he lost his balance and fell forward, knocking down a man and woman who had gone to help him. The soldier with the bandaged head ignored the confusion at his feet and shouted: "Where's Mary? Mary, where the hell are you, God damn you to hell."

"Here I am, John. Here I am," cried a woman in the crowd.

"Well, come and get me, God damn you, woman."

The crowd then realized that although the man's eyes were not covered, he was blind. The remaining civilian members of the fife and drum corps were on hand to escort the wounded men to their homes, but no one now thought of a welcoming parade. The fifers put their instruments back in their boots and the drummers slung their drums over their shoulders and soon the station platform was deserted.

The Private History of
a Campaign That Failed

MARK TWAIN

You have heard from a great many people who did something in the war,[1] is it not fair and right that you listen a little moment to one who started out to do something in it, but didn't? Thousands entered the war, got just a taste of it, and then stepped out again permanently. These, by their very numbers, are respectable and are therefore entitled to a sort of a voice—not a loud one but a modest one, not a boastful one but an apologetic one. They ought not to be allowed much space among better people—people who did something. I grant that, but they ought at least to be allowed to state why they didn't do anything and also to explain the process by which they didn't do anything. Surely this kind of light must have a sort of value.

Out West there was a good deal of confusion in men's minds during the first months of the great trouble —a good deal of unsettledness, of leaning first this way, then that, then the other way. It was hard for us to get our bearings. I call to mind an instance of this. I was piloting on the Mississippi when the news came that South Carolina had gone out of the Union on the 20th of December, 1860. My pilot mate was a New Yorker. He was strong for the Union; so was I. But he would not listen to me with any patience; my loyalty was

[1] In "Battles and Leaders of the Civil War," then running in the Century.—Ed.

smirched, to his eye, because my father had owned
slaves. I said in palliation of this dark fact that I had
heard my father say, some years before he died, that
slavery was a great wrong and that he would free the
solitary Negro he then owned if he could think it right
to give away the property of the family when he was so
straitened in means. My mate retorted that a mere impulse was nothing—anybody could pretend to a good
impulse, and went on decrying my Unionism and libel-
ing my ancestry. A month later the secession atmosphere had considerably thickened on the Lower Mississippi and I became a rebel; so did he. We were together
in New Orleans the 26th of January, when Louisiana
went out of the Union. He did his full share of the rebel
shouting but was bitterly opposed to letting me do
mine. He said that I came of bad stock—of a father who
had been willing to set slaves free. In the following
summer he was piloting a Federal gunboat and shouting for the Union again and I was in the Confederate
army. I held his note for some borrowed money. He
was one of the most upright men I ever knew but he
repudiated that note without hesitation because I was a
rebel and the son of a man who owned slaves.

In that summer of 1861 the first wash of the wave
of war broke upon the shores of Missouri. Our state was
invaded by the Union forces. They took possession of
St. Louis, Jefferson Barracks, and some other points. The
Governor, Claib Jackson, issued his proclamation calling
out fifty thousand militia to repel the invader.

I was visiting in the small town where my boyhood
had been spent, Hannibal, Marion County. Several of us
got together in a secret place by night and formed ourselves into a military company. One Tom Lyman, a
young fellow of a good deal of spirit but of no military
experience, was made captain; I was made second lieu-

tenant. We had no first lieutenant; I do not know why; it was long ago. There were fifteen of us. By the advice of an innocent connected with the organization we called ourselves the Marion Rangers. I do not remember that any one found fault with the name. I did not; I thought it sounded quite well. The young fellow who proposed this title was perhaps a fair sample of the kind of stuff we were made of. He was young, ignorant, good-natured, well-meaning, trivial, full of romance, and given to reading chivalric novels and singing forlorn love-ditties. He had some pathetic little nickel-plated aristocratic instincts and detested his name, which was Dunlap; detested it partly because it was nearly as common in that region as Smith but mainly because it had a plebeian sound to his ear. So he tried to ennoble it by writing it in this way: *d'Unlap*. That contented his eye but left his ear unsatisfied, for people gave the new name the same old pronunciation—emphasis on the front end of it. He then did the bravest thing that can be imagined, a thing to make one shiver when one remembers how the world is given to resenting shams and affectations, he began to write his name so: *d'Un Lap*. And he waited patiently through the long storm of mud that was flung at this work of art and he had his reward at last, for he lived to see that name accepted and the emphasis put where he wanted it by people who had known him all his life, and to whom the tribe of Dunlaps had been as familiar as the rain and the sunshine for forty years. So sure of victory at last is the courage that can wait. He said he had found by consulting some ancient French chronicles that the name was rightly and originally written d'Un Lap, and said that if it were translated into English it would mean Peterson: *Lap*, Latin or Greek, he said, for stone or rock, same as the French *pierre*, that is to say, Peter: *d'*, of or from; *un*, a or one; hence, d'Un Lap, of or from a stone or a Peter; that is to say, one who is the son of a stone, the son of a Peter—Peterson. Our militia company were not learned and the explanation confused them; so they called him Peterson Dunlap. He proved useful to us in his way; he named our camps for us and he generally struck a name that was "no slouch," as the boys said.

That is one sample of us. Another was Ed Stevens, son of the town jeweler, trim-built, handsome, graceful, neat as a cat; bright, educated, but given over entirely to fun. There was nothing serious in life to him. As far as he was concerned, this military expedition of ours was simply a holiday. I should say that about half of us looked upon it in the same way; not consciously, perhaps, but unconsciously. We did not think; we were not capable of it. As for myself, I was full of unreasoning joy to be done with turning out of bed at midnight and four in the morning for a while, grateful to have a change, new scenes, new occupations, a new interest. In my thoughts that was as far as I went; I did not go into the details; as a rule one doesn't at twenty-four.

Another sample was Smith, the blacksmith's apprentice. This vast donkey had some pluck, of a slow and sluggish nature, but a soft heart; at one time he would knock a horse down for some impropriety and at another he would get homesick and cry. However, he had one ultimate credit to his account which some of us hadn't; he stuck to the war and was killed in battle at last.

Jo Bowers, another sample, was a huge, good-natured, flax-headed lubber, lazy, sentimental, full of harmless brag, a grumbler by nature; an experienced, industrious, ambitious, and often quite picturesque liar and yet not a successful one, for he had had no intelligent training but was allowed to come up just any way.

This life was serious enough to him, and seldom satisfactory. But he was a good fellow, anyway, and the boys all liked him. He was made orderly sergeant; Stevens was made corporal.

These samples will answer—and they are quite fair ones. Well, this herd of cattle started for the war. What could you expect of them? They did as well as they knew how but, really, what was justly to be expected of them? Nothing, I should say. That is what they did.

We waited for a dark night, for caution and secrecy were necessary; then toward midnight we stole in couples and from various directions to the Griffith place, beyond the town; from that point we set out together on foot. Hannibal lies at the extreme southeastern corner of Marion County, on the Mississippi River; our objective point was the hamlet of New London, ten miles away, in Ralls County.

The first hour was all fun, all idle nonsense and laughter. But that could not be kept up. The steady trudging came to be like work, the play had somehow oozed out of it, the stillness of the woods and the somberness of the night began to throw a depressing influence over the spirits of the boys, and presently the talking died out and each person shut himself up in his own thoughts. During the last half of the second hour nobody said a word.

Now we approached a log farm-house where, according to report, there was a guard of five Union soldiers. Lyman called a halt and there, in the deep gloom of the overhanging branches, he began to whisper a plan of assault upon that house, which made the gloom more depressing than it was before. It was a crucial moment; we realized with a cold suddenness that here was no jest—we were standing face to face with actual war. We were equal to the occasion. In our response there was no hesitation, no indecision: we said that if Lyman wanted to meddle with those soldiers, he could go ahead and do it, but if he waited for us to follow him, he would wait a long time.

Lyman urged, pleaded, tried to shame us, but it had no effect. Our course was plain, our minds were made up: we would flank the farm-house—go out around. And that was what we did.

We struck into the woods and entered upon a rough time, stumbling over roots, getting tangled in vines and torn by briers. At last we reached an open place in a safe region and sat down, blown and hot, to cool off and nurse our scratches and bruises. Lyman was annoyed but the rest of us were cheerful; we had flanked the farm-house, we had made our first military movement and it was a success; we had nothing to fret about, we were feeling just the other way. Horse-play and laughing began again; the expedition was become a holiday frolic once more.

Then we had two more hours of dull trudging and ultimate silence and depression; then about dawn we straggled into New London, soiled, heel-blistered, fagged with our little march, and all of us except Stevens in a sour and raspy humor and privately down on the war. We stacked our shabby old shotguns in Colonel Ralls's barn and then went in a body and breakfasted with that veteran of the Mexican War. Afterward he took us to a distant meadow, and there in the shade of a tree we listened to an old-fashioned speech from him, full of gunpowder and glory, full of that adjective-piling, mixed metaphor and windy declamation which were regarded as eloquence in that ancient time and that remote region; and then he swore us on the Bible to be faithful to the State of Missouri and drive all invaders from her soil, no matter whence they might come or under what flag they might march. This mixed us considerably and we could not make out just what service we were embarked in, but Colonel Ralls, the practised politician and phrase-juggler, was not similarly in doubt; he knew quite clearly that he had invested us in the cause of the Southern Confederacy. He closed the solemnities by belting around me the sword which his neighbor, Colonel Brown, had worn at Buena Vista and Molino del Rey; and he accompanied this act with another impressive blast.

Then we formed in line of battle and marched four miles to a shady and pleasant piece of woods on the border of the far-reaching expanses of a flowery prairie. It was an enchanting region for war—our kind of war.

We pierced the forest about half a mile and took up a strong position, with some low, rocky, and wooded hills behind us and a purling, limpid creek in front. Straightway half the command were in swimming and the other half fishing. The ass with the French name gave this position a romantic title but it was too long, so the boys shortened and simplified it to Camp Ralls.

We occupied an old maple-sugar camp, whose half-rotted troughs were still propped against the trees. A long corn-crib served for sleeping-quarters for the battalion. On our left, half a mile away, were Mason's farm and house, and he was a friend to the cause. Shortly after noon the farmers began to arrive from several directions with mules and horses for our use, and these they lent us for as long as the war might last, which they judged would be about three months. The animals were of all sizes, all colors, and all breeds. They were mainly young and frisky, and nobody in the command could stay on them long at a time, for we were town boys and ignorant of horsemanship. The creature that fell to my share was a very small mule, and yet so quick

and active that it could throw me without difficulty, and
it did this whenever I got on it. Then it would bray—
stretching its neck out, laying its ears back, and spreading its jaws till you could see down to its works. It was
a disagreeable animal in every way. If I took it by the
bridle and tried to lead it off the grounds, it would sit
down and brace back and no one could budge it. However, I was not entirely destitute of military resources
and I did presently manage to spoil this game, for I had
seen many a steamboat aground in my time and knew a
trick or two which even a grounded mule would be
obliged to respect. There was a well by the corn-crib; so
I substituted thirty fathom of rope for the bridle, and
fetched him home with the windlass.

I will anticipate here sufficiently to say that we did
learn to ride after some days' practice, but never well.
We could not learn to like our animals; they were not
choice ones and most of them had annoying peculiari-
ties of one kind or another. Stevens's horse would carry
him, when he was not noticing, under the huge excres-
cences which form on the trunks of oak-trees, and wipe
him out of the saddle; in this way Stevens got several
bad hurts. Sergeant Bowers's horse was very large and
tall, with slim, long legs, and looked like a railroad
bridge. His size enabled him to reach all about, and as
far as he wanted to, with his head; so he was always
biting Bowers's legs. On the march, in the sun, Bowers
slept a good deal, and as soon as the horse recognized
that he was asleep he would reach around and bite him
on the leg. His legs were black and blue with bites. This
was the only thing that could ever make him swear but
this always did; whenever his horse bit him he always
swore, and of course Stevens, who laughed at everything, laughed at this and would even get into such
convulsions over it as to lose his balance and fall off his

horse; and then Bowers, already irritated by the pain of the horse-bite, would resent the laughter with hard language, and there would be a quarrel; so that horse made no end of trouble and bad blood in the command.

However, I will get back to where I was—our first afternoon in the sugar-camp. The sugar-troughs came very handy as horse-troughs and we had plenty of corn to fill them with. I ordered Sergeant Bowers to feed my mule, but he said that if I reckoned he went to war to be a dry-nurse to a mule it wouldn't take me very long to find out my mistake. I believed that this was insubordination but I was full of uncertainties about everything military, and so I let the thing pass and went and ordered Smith, the blacksmith's apprentice, to feed the mule; but he merely gave me a large, cold, sarcastic grin, such as an ostensibly seven-year-old horse gives you when you lift his lip and find he is fourteen, and turned his back on me. I then went to the captain and asked if it were not right and proper and military for me to have an orderly. He said it was but as there was only one orderly in the corps, it was but right that he himself should have Bowers on his staff. Bowers said he wouldn't serve on anybody's staff, and if anybody thought he could make him, let him try it. So, of course, the thing had to be dropped; there was no other way.

Next, nobody would cook; it was considered a degradation; so we had no dinner. We lazied the rest of the pleasant afternoon away, some dozing under the trees, some smoking cob-pipes and talking sweethearts and war, some playing games. By late supper-time all hands were famished and to meet the difficulty all hands turned to on an equal footing, and gathered wood, built fires, and cooked the meal. Afterward everything was smooth for a while; then trouble broke out between the corporal and the sergeant, each claiming to rank the

other. Nobody knew which was the higher office; so
Lyman had to settle the matter by making the rank of
both officers equal. The commander of an ignorant crew
like that has many troubles and vexations which probably do not occur in the regular army at all. However,
with the song-singing and yarn-spinning around the
camp-fire, everything presently became serene again,
and by and by we raked the corn down level in one end
of the crib and all went to bed on it, tying a horse to the
door, so that he would neigh if any one tried to get in.[1]

We had some horsemanship drill every forenoon;
then, afternoons, we rode off here and there in squads a
few miles and visited the farmers' girls, and had a
youthful good time and got an honest good dinner or
supper, and then home again to camp, happy and content.

For a time life was idly delicious, it was perfect;
there was nothing to mar it. Then came some farmers
with an alarm one day. They said it was rumored that
the enemy were advancing in our direction from over
Hyde's prairie. The result was a sharp stir among us,
and general consternation. It was a rude awakening
from our pleasant trance. The rumor was but a rumor—
nothing definite about it; so in the confusion we did not
know which way to retreat. Lyman was for not retreating at all in these uncertain circumstances, but he found
that if he tried to maintain that attitude he would fare
badly, for the command were in no humor to put up

[1] It was always my impression that that was what the horse was there for
and I know that it was also the impression of at least one other of the command, for we talked about it at the time and admired the military ingenuity
of the device; but when I was out West three years ago, I was told by Mr.
A. G. Fuqua, a member of our company, that the horse was his, that the
leaving him tied at the door was a matter of mere forgetfulness, and that to
attribute it to intelligent invention was to give him quite too much credit. In
support of his position he called my attention to the suggestive fact that the
artifice was not employed again. I had not thought of that before.

with insubordination. So he yielded the point and called
a council of war, to consist of himself and the three
other officers; but the privates made such a fuss about
being left out that we had to allow them to remain, for
they were already present and doing the most of the
talking too. The question was, which way to retreat; but
all were so flurried that nobody seemed to have even a
guess to offer. Except Lyman. He explained in a few
calm words that, inasmuch as the enemy were approaching from over Hyde's prairie, our course was
simple: all we had to do was not to retreat *toward* him;
any other direction would answer our needs perfectly.
Everybody saw in a moment how true this was, and
how wise, so Lyman got a great many compliments. It
was now decided that we should fall back on Mason's
farm.

It was after dark by this time and as we could not
know how soon the enemy might arrive, it did not seem
best to try to take the horses and things with us; so we
only took the guns and ammunition, and started at
once. The route was very rough and hilly and rocky,
and presently the night grew very black and rain began
to fall; so we had a troublesome time of it, struggling
and stumbling along in the dark, and soon some person
slipped and fell, and then the next person behind stumbled over him and fell, and so did the rest, one after the
other; and then Bowers came, with the keg of powder in
his arms, while the command were all mixed together,
arms and legs, on the muddy slope, and so he fell, of
course, with the keg, and this started the whole detachment down the hill in a body, and they landed in the
brook at the bottom in a pile, and each that was under-
most pulling the hair and scratching and biting those
that were on top of him, and those that were being
scratched and bitten scratching and biting the rest in

their turn, and all saying they would die before they would ever go to war again if they ever got out of this brook this time and the invader might rot for all they cared, and the country along with him—and all such talk as that, which was dismal to hear and take part in, in such smothered, low voices, and such a grisly dark place and so wet, and the enemy, maybe, coming any moment.

The keg of powder was lost, and the guns too; so the growling and complaining continued straight along while the brigade pawed around the pasty hillside and slopped around in the brook hunting for these things; consequently we lost considerable time at this, and then we heard a sound and held our breath and listened, and it seemed to be the enemy coming, though it could have been a cow, for it had a cough like a cow; but we did not wait but left a couple of guns behind and struck out for Mason's again as briskly as we could scramble along in the dark. But we got lost presently among the rugged little ravines and wasted a deal of time finding the way again, so it was after nine when we reached Mason's stile at last; and then before we could open our mouths to give the countersign several dogs came bounding over the fence with great riot and noise, and each of them took a soldier by the slack of his trousers and began to back away with him. We could not shoot the dogs without endangering the persons they were attached to; so we had to look on helpless at what was perhaps the most mortifying spectacle of the Civil War. There was light enough and to spare, for the Masons had now run out on the porch with candles in their hands. The old man and his son came and undid the dogs without difficulty, all but Bowers's; but they couldn't undo his dog, they didn't know his combination; he was of the bull kind and seemed to be set with a

Yale time-lock, but they got him loose at last with some scalding water, of which Bowers got his share and returned thanks. Peterson Dunlap afterward made up a fine name for this engagement, and also for the night march which preceded it, but both have long ago faded out of my memory.

We now went into the house and they began to ask us a world of questions, whereby it presently came out that we did not know anything concerning who or what we were running from; so the old gentleman made himself very frank and said we were a curious breed of soldiers and guessed we could be depended on to end up the war in time, because no government could stand the expense of the shoe-leather we should cost it trying to follow us around. "Marion *Rangers!* good name, b'gosh!" said he. And wanted to know why we hadn't had a picket-guard at the place where the road entered the prairie, and why we hadn't sent out a scouting party to spy out the enemy and bring us an account of his strength, and so on, before jumping up and stampeding out of a strong position upon a mere vague rumor—and so on, and so forth, till he made us all feel shabbier than the dogs had done, not half so enthusiastically welcome. So we went to bed shamed and low-spirited, except Stevens. Soon Stevens began to devise a garment for Bowers which could be made to automatically display his battle-scars to the grateful or conceal them from the envious, according to his occasions, but Bowers was in no humor for this, so there was a fight and when it was over Stevens had some battle-scars of his own to think about.

Then we got a little sleep. But after all we had gone through, our activities were not over for the night, for about two o'clock in the morning we heard a shout of warning from down the lane, accompanied by a chorus from all the dogs, and in a moment everybody was up and flying around to find out what the alarm was about. The alarmist was a horseman who gave notice that a detachment of Union soldiers was on its way from Hannibal with orders to capture and hang any bands like ours which it could find, and said we had no time to lose. Farmer Mason was in a flurry this time himself. He hurried us out of the house with all haste, and sent one of his Negroes with us to show us where to hide ourselves and our telltale guns among the ravines half a mile away. It was raining heavily.

We struck down the lane, then across some rocky pasture-land which offered good advantages for stumbling; consequently we were down in the mud most of the time, and every time a man went down he blackguarded the war and the people that started it and everybody connected with it, and gave himself the master dose of all for being so foolish as to go into it. At last we reached the wooded mouth of a ravine, and there we huddled ourselves under the streaming trees and sent the Negro back home. It was a dismal and heart-breaking time. We were like to be drowned with the rain, deafened with the howling wind and the booming thunder, and blinded by the lightning. It was indeed a wild night. The drenching we were getting was misery enough, but a deeper misery still was the reflection that the halter might end us before we were a day older. A death of this shameful sort had not occurred to us as being among the possibilities of war. It took the romance all out of the campaign and turned our dreams of glory into a repulsive nightmare. As for doubting that so barbarous an order had been given, not one of us did that.

The long night wore itself out at last, and then the Negro came to us with the news that the alarm had manifestly been a false one and that breakfast would soon be ready. Straightway we were light-hearted again, and the world was bright and life as full of hope and promise as ever—for we were young then. How long ago that was! Twenty-four years.

The mongrel child of philology named the night's refuge Camp Devastation and no soul objected. The Masons gave us a Missouri country breakfast in Missourian abundance, and we needed it: hot biscuits, hot "wheat bread," prettily criss-crossed in a lattice pattern on top, hot corn-pone, fried chicken, bacon, coffee, eggs, milk, buttermilk, etc., and the world may be confidently challenged to furnish the equal of such a breakfast, as it is cooked in the South.

We stayed several days at Mason's, and after all these years the memory of the dullness and stillness and lifelessness of that slumberous farm-house still oppresses my spirit as with a sense of the presence of death and mourning. There was nothing to do, nothing to think about; there was no interest in life. The male part of the household were away in the fields all day, the women were busy and out of our sight; there was no sound but the plaintive wailing of a spinning-wheel, forever moaning out from some distant room, the most lonesome sound in nature, a sound steeped and sodden with homesickness and the emptiness of life. The family went to bed about dark every night, and as we were not invited to intrude any new customs we naturally followed theirs. Those nights were a hundred years long to youths accustomed to being up till twelve. We lay awake and miserable till that hour every time, and grew old and decrepit waiting through the still eternities for the clock-strikes. This was no place for town boys. So at last it was with something very like joy that we received news that the enemy were on our track again. With a new birth of the old warrior spirit we sprang to our places in line of battle and fell back on Camp Ralls.

Captain Lyman had taken a hint from Mason's talk, and he now gave orders that our camp should be guarded against surprise by the posting of pickets. I was ordered to place a picket at the forks of the road in Hyde's prairie. Night shut down black and threatening. I told Sergeant Bowers to go out to that place and stay till midnight and, just as I was expecting, he said he wouldn't do it. I tried to get others to go but all refused. Some excused themselves on account of the weather, but the rest were frank enough to say they wouldn't go in any kind of weather. This kind of thing sounds odd now, and impossible, but there was no surprise in it at the time. On the contrary, it seemed a perfectly natural thing to do. There were scores of little camps scattered over Missouri where the same thing was happening. These camps were composed of young men who had been born and reared to a sturdy independence, and who did not know what it meant to be ordered around by Tom, Dick, and Harry, whom they had known familiarly all their lives in the village or on the farm. It is quite within the probabilities that this same thing was happening all over the South. James Redpath recognized the justice of this assumption and furnished the following instance in support of it. During a short stay in East Tennessee he was in a citizen colonel's tent one day talking, when a big private appeared at the door and, without salute or other circumlocution, said to the colonel:

"Say, Jim, I'm a-goin' home for a few days."

"What for?"

"Well, I hain't b'en there for a right smart while and I'd like to see how things is comin' on."

"How long are you going to be gone?"

" 'Bout two weeks."

"Well, don't be gone longer than that, and get back sooner if you can."

That was all, and the citizen officer resumed his conversation where the private had broken it off. This was in the first months of the war, of course. The camps in our part of Missouri were under Brigadier-General Thomas H. Harris. He was a townsman of ours, a first-rate fellow and well liked, but we had all familiarly known him as the sole and modest-salaried operator in our telegraph-office, where he had to send about one despatch a week in ordinary times and two when there was a rush of business; consequently, when he appeared in our midst one day on the wing, and delivered a military command of some sort in a large military fashion, nobody was surprised at the response which he got from the assembled soldiery:

"Oh, now, what'll you take to *don't*, Tom Harris?"

It was quite the natural thing. One might justly imagine that we were hopeless material for war. And so we seemed in our ignorant state, but there were those among us who afterward learned the grim trade, learned to obey like machines, became valuable soldiers; fought all through the war, and came out at the end with excellent records. One of the very boys who refused to go out on picket duty that night and called me an ass for thinking he would expose himself to danger in such a foolhardy way, had become distinguished for intrepidity before he was a year older.

I did secure my picket that night, not by authority but by diplomacy. I got Bowers to go by agreeing to exchange ranks with him for the time being, and go along and stand the watch with him as his subordinate. We stayed out there a couple of dreary hours in the pitchy darkness and the rain, with nothing to modify the dreariness but Bowers's monotonous growlings at the war and the weather; then we began to nod and presently found it next to impossible to stay in the saddle, so we gave up the tedious job and went back to the camp without waiting for the relief guard. We rode into camp without interruption or objection from anybody and the enemy could have done the same, for there were no sentries. Everybody was asleep; at midnight there was nobody to send out another picket, so none was sent. We never tried to establish a watch at night again, as far as I remember, but we generally kept a picket out in the daytime.

In that camp the whole command slept on the corn in the big corn-crib and there was usually a general row before morning, for the place was full of rats and they would scramble over the boys' bodies and faces, annoying and irritating everybody, and now and then they would bite some one's toe, and the person who owned the toe would start up and magnify his English and begin to throw corn in the dark. The ears were half as heavy as bricks and when they struck they hurt. The persons struck would respond and inside of five minutes every man would be locked in a death-grip with his neighbor. There was a grievous deal of blood shed in the corn-crib but this was all that was spilt while I was in the war. No, that is not quite true. But for one circumstance it would have been all. I will come to that now.

Our scares were frequent. Every few days rumors would come that the enemy were approaching. In these cases we always fell back on some other camp of ours; we never stayed where we were. But the rumors always turned out to be false, so at last even we began to grow indifferent to them. One night a Negro was sent to our corn-crib with the same old warning, the enemy was hovering in our neighborhood. We all said let him hover. We resolved to stay still and be comfortable. It was a fine warlike resolution, and no doubt we all felt the stir of it in our veins—for a moment. We had been having a very jolly time, that was full of horse-play and schoolboy hilarity, but that cooled down now and presently the fast-waning fire of forced jokes and forced laughs died out altogether and the company became silent. Silent and nervous. And soon uneasy—worried—apprehensive. We had said we would stay and we were committed. We could have been persuaded to go but there was nobody brave enough to suggest it. An almost noiseless movement presently began in the dark by a general but unvoiced impulse. When the movement was completed each man knew that he was not the only person who had crept to the front wall and had his eye at a crack between the logs. No, we were all there, all there with our hearts in our throats and staring out toward the sugar-troughs where the forest footpath came through. It was late and there was a deep woodsy stillness everywhere. There was a veiled moonlight, which was only just strong enough to enable us to mark the general shape of objects. Presently a muffled sound caught our ears and we recognized it as the hoof-beats of a horse or horses. And right away a figure appeared in the forest path; it could have been made of smoke, its mass had so little sharpness of outline. It was a man on horseback and it seemed to me that there were others behind him. I got hold of a gun in the dark, and pushed it through a crack between the logs, hardly knowing what I was doing, I was so dazed with fright. Somebody said "Fire!" I pulled the trigger. I seemed to see a hundred flashes and hear a hundred reports; then I saw the man fall down out of the saddle. My first feeling was of surprised gratification; my first impulse was an apprentice-sportsman's impulse to run and pick up his game. Somebody said, hardly audibly, "Good—we've got him!—wait for the rest." But the rest did not come. We waited—listened—still no more came. There was not a sound, not the whisper of a leaf; just perfect stillness, an uncanny kind of stillness which was all the more uncanny on account of the damp, earthy, late-night smells now rising and pervading it. Then, wondering, we crept stealthily out and approached the man. When we got to him the moon revealed him distinctly. He was lying on his back with his arms abroad, his mouth was open and his chest heaving with long gasps, and his white shirt-front was all splashed with blood. The thought shot through me that I was a murderer, that I had killed a man, a man who had never done me any harm. That was the coldest sensation that ever went through my marrow. I was down by him in a moment, helplessly stroking his forehead, and I would have given anything then—my own life freely—to make him again what he had been five minutes before. And all the boys seemed to be feeling in the same way; they hung over him, full of pitying interest, and tried all they could to help him and said all sorts of regretful things. They had forgotten all about the enemy, they thought only of this one forlorn unit of the foe. Once my imagination persuaded me that the dying man gave me a reproachful look out of his shadowy eyes, and it seemed to me that I could rather he had stabbed me than done that. He muttered and mumbled like a dreamer in his sleep about his wife and his child, and I thought with a new despair, "This thing that I have done does not end with him; it falls upon *them* too, and they never did me any harm, any more than he."

In a little while the man was dead. He was killed in war, killed in fair and legitimate war, killed in battle, as you may say, and yet he was as sincerely mourned by the opposing force as if he had been their brother. The boys stood there a half-hour sorrowing over him and recalling the details of the tragedy, and wondering who he might be and if he were a spy, and saying that if it were to do over again they would not hurt him unless he attacked them first. It soon came out that mine was not the only shot fired; there were five others, a division of the guilt which was a great relief to me since it in some degree lightened and diminished the burden I was carrying. There were six shots fired at once but I was not in my right mind at the time, and my heated imagination had magnified my one shot into a volley.

The man was not in uniform and was not armed. He was a stranger in the country, that was all we ever found out about him. The thought of him got to preying upon me every night; I could not get rid of it. I could not drive it away, the taking of that unoffending life seemed such a wanton thing. And it seemed an epitome of war, that all war must be just that the killing of strangers against whom you feel no personal animosity, strangers whom in other circumstances you would help if you found them in trouble, and who would help you if you needed it. My campaign was spoiled. It seemed to me that I was not rightly equipped for this awful business, that war was intended for men and I for a child's nurse. I resolved to retire from this avocation of sham soldiership while I could save some remnant of my self-respect. These morbid thoughts clung to me against reason, for at bottom I did not believe I had touched that man. The law of probabilities decreed me guiltless of his blood for in all my small experience with guns I had never hit anything I had tried to hit and I knew I had done my best to hit him. Yet there was no solace in the thought. Against a diseased imagination demonstration goes for nothing.

The rest of my war experience was of a piece with what I have already told of it. We kept monotonously falling back upon one camp or another and eating up the farmers and their families. They ought to have shot us; on the contrary, they were as hospitably kind and courteous to us as if we had deserved it. In one of these camps we found Ab Grimes, an Upper Mississippi pilot who afterward became famous as a dare-devil rebel spy, whose career bristled with desperate adventures. The look and style of his comrades suggested that they had not come into the war to play and their deeds made good the conjecture later. They were fine horsemen and good revolver shots, but their favorite arm was the lasso. Each had one at his pommel and could snatch a man out of the saddle with it every time, on a full gallop, at any reasonable distance.

In another camp the chief was a fierce and profane old blacksmith of sixty and he had furnished his twenty recruits with gigantic home-made bowie-knives, to be swung with two hands like the *machetes* of the Isthmus. It was a grisly spectacle to see that earnest band practising their murderous cuts and slashes under the eye of that remorseless old fanatic.

The last camp which we fell back upon was in a hollow near the village of Florida where I was born, in Monroe County. Here we were warned one day that a Union colonel was sweeping down on us with a whole regiment at his heel. This looked decidedly serious. Our boys went apart and consulted; then we went back and told the other companies present that the war was a disappointment to us and we were going to disband. They were getting ready themselves to fall back on some place or other, and we were only waiting for General Tom Harris, who was expected to arrive at any moment, so they tried to persuade us to wait a little while but the majority of us said no, we were accustomed to falling back and didn't need any of Tom Harris's help, we could get along perfectly well without him and save time, too. So about half of our fifteen, including myself, mounted and left on the instant; the others yielded to persuasion and stayed—stayed through the war.

An hour later we met General Harris on the road, with two or three people in his company, his staff probably, but we could not tell; none of them were in uniform; uniforms had not come into vogue among us yet. Harris ordered us back but we told him there was a Union colonel coming with a whole regiment in his wake and it looked as if there was going to be a disturbance, so we had concluded to go home. He raged a little but it was of no use, our minds were made up. We had done our share, had killed one man, exterminated one army, such as it was; let him go and kill the rest and that would end the war. I did not see that brisk young general again until last year; then he was wearing white hair and whiskers.

In time I came to know that Union colonel whose coming frightened me out of the war and crippled the Southern cause to that extent—General Grant. I came within a few hours of seeing him when he was as unknown as I was myself; at a time when anybody could have said, "Grant?—Ulysses S. Grant? I do not remember hearing the name before." It seems difficult to realize that there was once a time when such a remark could be rationally made but there *was*, and I was within a few miles of the place and the occasion too, though proceeding in the other direction.

The thoughtful will not throw this war paper of mine lightly aside as being valueless. It has this value: it is a not unfair picture of what went on in many and many a militia camp in the first months of the rebellion, when the green recruits were without discipline, without the steadying and heartening influence of trained leaders, when all their circumstances were new and strange and charged with exaggerated terrors, and before the invaluable experience of actual collision in the field had turned them from rabbits into soldiers. If this side of the picture of that early day has not before been put into history, then history has been to that degree incomplete, for it had and has its rightful place there. There was more Bull Run material scattered through the early camps of this country than exhibited itself at Bull Run. And yet it learned its trade presently and helped to fight the great battles later. I could have become a soldier myself if I had waited. I had got part of it learned, I knew more about retreating than the man that invented retreating.

Second Inaugural

ABRAHAM LINCOLN

Washington, D. C.
March 4, 1865

Fellow-Countrymen: At this second appearing to take the oath of the Presidential office there is less occasion for an extended address than there was at the first. Then a statement somewhat in detail of a course to be pursued seemed fitting and proper. Now, at the expiration of four years, during which public declarations have been constantly called forth on every point and phase of the great contest which still absorbs the attention and engrosses the energies of the nation, little that is new could be presented. The progress of our arms, upon which all else chiefly depends, is as well known to the public as to myself, and it is, I trust, reasonably satisfactory and encouraging to all. With high hope for the future, no prediction in regard to it is ventured.

On the occasion corresponding to this four years ago all thoughts were anxiously directed to an impending civil war. All dreaded it, all sought to avert it. While the inaugural address was being delivered from this place, devoted altogether to saving the Union without war, insurgent agents were in the city seeking to destroy it without war—seeking to dissolve the Union and divide effects by negotiation. Both parties deprecated war, but one of them would make war rather than let the nation survive; and the other would accept war rather than let it perish. And the war came.

One eighth of the whole population were colored slaves, not distributed generally over the Union but localized in the southern part of it. These slaves constituted a peculiar and powerful interest. All knew that this interest was somehow the cause of the war. To strengthen, perpetuate, and extend this interest was the object for which the insurgents would rend the Union, even by war; while the government claimed no right to do more than to restrict the territorial enlargement of it.

Neither party expected for the war the magnitude or the duration which it has already attained. Neither anticipated that the cause of the conflict might cease when, or even before, the conflict itself should cease. Each looked for an easier triumph, and a result less fundamental and astounding. Both read the same Bible and pray to the same God, and each invokes His aid against the other. It may seem strange that any men should dare to ask a just God's assistance in wringing their bread from the sweat of other men's faces, but let us judge not, that we be not judged. The prayers of both could not be answered—that of neither has been answered fully.

The Almighty has His own purposes. "Woe unto the world because of offenses; for it must needs be that offenses come, but woe to that man by whom the offense cometh." If we shall suppose that American slavery is one of those offenses which, in the providence of God, must needs come, but which, having continued through His appointed time, He now wills to remove, and that He gives to both North and South this terrible war as the woe due to those by whom the offense came, shall we discern therein any departure from those divine attributes which the believers in a living God always ascribe to Him? Fondly do we hope, fervently do we pray, that this mighty scourge of war may speedily pass away. Yet, if God wills that it continue until all the wealth piled by the bondsman's two hundred and fifty years of unrequited toil shall be sunk, and until every drop of blood drawn with the lash shall be paid by another drawn with the sword, as was said three thousand years ago, so still it must be said "the judgments of the Lord are true and righteous altogether."

With malice toward none, with charity for all, with firmness in the right, as God gives us to see the right, let us strive on to finish the work we are in, to bind up the nation's wounds, to care for him who shall have borne the battle and for his widow and his orphan—to do all which may achieve and cherish a just and lasting peace among ourselves and with all nations.